D1524153

More Than a Survivor

A Child's Story of War, Loss, and Joy

Fatu Koroma Litsey

DEDICATION

To my grandmother. You were like a mother to me. Thank you
for the love you showed me as a little girl. I am sorry that you
didn't get to watch me grow up into a young lady. I am sorry you
had to let me go in order for me to have a better life. During the
few years I was with you, you taught me how to work hard and
how to love people. I hope to see you again someday.

CONTENTS

ACKNOWLEDGMENTS

I want to thank my parents for encouraging me to share my story with the world and for helping me shape it into a book. Thank you, Mom and Dad, for adopting three girls from Africa and showing us what it means to follow Christ. I also want to thank my brother William for using his amazing talent to create the cover of this book. Finally, I want to thank all my brothers and sisters, Matt, Rachel, Laura, Jack, and William, for making room in your hearts for Sinnah, Sento, and me.

"I have told you these things, so that in me you may have peace. In this world you will have trouble. But take heart! I have overcome the world."

-JESUS, IN THE GOSPEL OF JOHN

INTRODUCTION

People sometimes ask me if I was born with only one hand. I always tell them no.

My name is Fatu. I was born in a small village in a West African country called Sierra Leone. When I was a little girl my country experienced a very bad civil war. My life changed forever the day the war came to my village. I want to tell you my story.

Please understand that some of these events occurred while I was a young child. I will describe them exactly as I remember them, but that may not be exactly the way they happened.

Some of these things will be difficult to read. But I am not writing so that you will pity me. The hero of my story isn't me. The hero of my story is God. He is the one who took evil and worked good from it. I hope that reading my story will help you see how God is working in your life too.

MAFUNTA

Try to imagine living in a village where communication with the rest of the world barely exists. A village where there is little outside information, no landlines or cell phones, no newspapers, no radios, no computers, and no televisions. A village where people only know what is happening right there at that moment. I used to live in a village like that. It was the start of my life, so my story will start there as well.

My village was called Mafunta. I can't really tell you the population, maybe several dozen. Everybody knew everybody else. When I was living there, I spoke Timni. That was the language that everyone in Mafunta spoke. Let me tell you what Mafunta was like before the war came to us.

We lived a simple life, but to me it seemed a good life. Each family had their own plot of land to farm and we all worked together to plant and help gather the food. Until the war came to us, we lived a peaceful life. The only things we feared were snakes and wild animals.

We grew food in our fields: rice, peanuts, peppers, okra, cucumbers, corn, tomatoes, cassava, pineapples, and beans. We had trees full of mangoes, avocados, bananas, oranges, papayas, cashews, coconuts, and palm nuts. Kids growing up in our village had no problem finding food. There were all types of fruits and plants to eat.

One of our main foods was cassava. It could grow in just about any dry soil. We could eat its roots and leaves. The roots could be eaten uncooked, fresh from the ground, or cooked and eaten with a sauce made of cassava leaves or peanuts. From the roots of the cassava, we made "fufu". The way I remember making fufu was to soak the peeled roots for a couple of days until they produced a certain aroma. We would lay them out in the sun to dry for a day or so, then pound them into really fine flour. The flour was cooked by adding water into the pot while stirring until it produced a thick, sticky, fluffy food that we ate with different sauces. I loved fufu, but making it was not easy. Stirring the pot could

4

make even a strong woman's arms tired!

There weren't any stoves in Mafunta. We cooked all our food over wood fires. The ladies would start a fire between three rocks, then they would balance their big cooking pots over the rocks above the fire. They used long wooden spoons so they could stand while they stirred the food as it cooked. As the fire burned they would push sticks between the rocks into the fire. They could control the heat of the fire by pushing the sticks in or pulling the sticks out. We kids were always the ones to collect wood for the fires. Cooking a meal in Mafunta was not easy!

Palm trees were another really good food source. We didn't plant them. They just grew on their own. I remember following my grandmother with the men who were going to climb the tree to retrieve the clusters of palm nuts. I used to love watching the men climb the palm trees. They could climb the trees really fast, using only hand-made ropes made out of tough vines. They wrapped the rope around the trunk, then leaned back into the rope and used their legs to climb. They would stick an ax into the tree above their heads, climb up to it, then unhook the ax and strike the tree above their heads again. They would continue this until they reached the top of the palm tree.

It was fun watching from below as they cut the palm nut clusters and let them drop to the ground. I remember being so excited as I watched each one fall. We kids would gather the clusters and any loose palm nuts.

We could eat palm nuts uncooked. Every time a cluster landed, I and the other kids would help ourselves to some. There were two ways of eating palm nuts. One way was to chew the seeds, which left an oily taste in our mouths. Another way was to crack them open. The kernel inside looked like the inside of a coconut. We would chew this kernel for the creamy taste. When the seeds from the palm trees were ripe, they would fall to the ground all on their own. There weren't a lot of them, but enough for us to eat throughout the day.

The most exciting part about harvesting palm nuts, though, was turning them into palm oil. We had a really big pot that was used just for that. The way I remember it, we would separate the nuts from the clusters then the adult ladies would put all the nuts in that big pot full of boiling water. They would let them boil for a while and after that the real fun would begin.

We had a big cement-lined pit that we used to mash the cooked nuts. On one side of the pit was a hole that was blocked off with balls of papaya leaves so water couldn't escape. The hot seeds were put into the pit. Some of the ladies would get in and start walking around the pit mashing the nuts. Before they would get in, they would always tie their long skirts up to their knees. We kids would carry water from the lake to pour into the pit. We would go back and forth many times to get water, while laughing at the adult ladies as they danced around on the hot palm nuts. As soon as the nuts cooled, other ladies and teenagers would take over carrying water and we kids would jump in to help mash the nuts. I remember running around in the pit playing catch. We were usually not in the pit for very long before the pit would be half-way filled and the red palm oil would start to rise up. Soon all the kids would get out of the pit because the water would be too high for us. I remember our legs would be covered in shiny red palm oil up to our thighs.

Once out, we would help gather the oil. We would lean over the edge of the pit with a wooden bowl and scoop up the oil. A couple of us would always lean too far and fall head first into the pit. When someone retrieved us, our bodies would be covered in the red oil! After all the oil had been collected, it was put into the big pot again to be reheated until it became richer and darker. Once the water had been emptied from the pit, we would gather the nuts that were left on the bottom and place them in a pile. Anyone could go to the pile to crack them and eat the kernels. I remember there used to be a big rock and a little rock right by the pile. We kids would argue over who got to use the big rock, although there were rocks everywhere!

Not only did we use palm oil for eating, we also used it as lotion. I remember at the end of each day, all the kids would run to the lake and the mothers would follow to wash. The mothers and children were at one end of the lake and the men were at the other. My grandmother would wash me before she washed herself. Then she would rub palm oil all over my skin and even in my hair. I used to love the smell of it on my skin.

The village men hunted for meat with spears and bows and arrows. They also knew how to set traps to catch animals. Sometimes they would bring a trap back with an animal still alive inside. I remember watching each time as they killed the animals. The animals would always try to fight them. It was not a pretty thing to watch.

For us kids, the most exciting traps were the ones for crabs. Every night before we went back to the village, the men would place the crab traps in the lake near our farm. They put rocks in the traps so they would sink. When we came back the next morning, the ladies would pull the traps out to see what was inside. They would carry the traps back to the farm on their heads. We carried many things on our heads, whether light or heavy! When we saw them coming with the traps we kids would run to help, because in the trap there would be so many creatures: fish flopping around, shrimp snapping their tails, snails lying there not moving at all, and crabs climbing the walls and snapping constantly. We were more interested in the crabs than in anything else. We enjoyed teasing them, poking at them to try to get them to snap at us. The game was to see who could get their finger closest to the crab without getting snapped. One of us would always get pinched and run around screaming, crying and waving his hand up in the air with the crab still holding on. We would all laugh and laugh, and that's usually when the game would end.

We made our own clothes too. I remember the older ladies sitting in a circle pounding dye into cloth with wooden mallets over and over. They would talk loudly to hear themselves over the heavy pounding and laugh as they joked around with each other. When they were done, the ground would be colored with different dyes. Then they would lay the brightly colored cloth on the grass to dry. It was a beautiful sight.

Even though there was no school in Mafunta,

I learned a lot as a child. Most of the things I learned were physical. For example, at a young age, I learned how to carry pails of water on my head to water the plants. It wasn't easy, but I became so good that I could carry gallons of water on my head with no hands while eating peanuts at the same time! We all could.

Learning how to fish using only buckets and nets wasn't easy, but it was fun! I used to love going fishing with the adult ladies. We would use big rocks and logs to block off an area of the lake. We then would use buckets to remove water from the enclosure. Once most of the water was out, only mud and fish would be left. We would catch them with our bare hands or nets and throw them in the buckets. Once in a while, there would be a water snake among the fish and things would get interesting! Everyone would grab a stick or a rock to help kill it. We were afraid of all snakes. We didn't play with them, but killed every one we saw because we could never tell which snake was poisonous.

My favorite part about fishing was catching electric fish. I don't remember what they were called in my language. I just remember how excited all the kids were every time we caught one. We would hold it to get that electric feeling running up our arms. We would always hesitate to touch it, but once we did, we would laugh and laugh at ourselves while it shocked us!

I learned how to plant rice alongside the adults. That was something I enjoyed very much. To plant rice, you must have a field that is muddy. I used to love walking into the high mud copying everything the adults did. That's how we learned, by copying the adults.

It was a lot of hard work, planting rice. There was a lot of bending down for long periods of time. I remember working alongside my grand-mother. She always made a loud cry as she stood up to stretch her lower back. She would then look down at me and smile before bending over to work again. Planting rice wasn't as hard for the kids as it was for the adults. We didn't have to bend so far! When the day of planting was over, my face and clothing would be covered in mud. We kids couldn't work without having any fun, so whenever the adults were too busy to notice, we would throw mud at each other and stomp around to see who could make the biggest splash.

It took a while for the rice to mature, at least a couple of months. When it finally did, it was so beautiful to look out over the fields and see the yellow heads of rice dancing happily in the wind. It was so peaceful hearing the swishing sound of their dance. And I remember the wonderful aroma of a field of rice ready for harvest.

On the day of the rice harvest, the men would cut the stalks of rice with curved sickles and the ladies would follow, gathering the stalks and tying them together. As a kid, our job was to gather the bundles and place them in a big pile. I remember going behind my grandmother trying to gather together as many of the bundles as my little hands could carry, so I could keep up with her. It wasn't easy, because she was fast at tying the bundles together. It was hard work but fun.

One part I didn't like, though. I spent most of the time scratching myself. Every time I would carry a bundle close to my skin I would itch like crazy. My whole body would be covered in tiny bumps that I couldn't help scratching. When the sun got too hot to work we would stop to rest. I remember my grandmother would cover my body with a white paste. All the other kids got the same treatment and we would all walk around looking like ghosts. It helped with the itching, but it was very hard to remove. Usually my grandmother would wash me in the lake at the end of the day. She used to lather soap all over my body using only her hands then pour water over me. But when I had the white paste on my skin she used a cloth, and scrubbed me so hard that I would cry.

Each day, after we brought the bundles in

from the field, we would separate the rice from the stalks. To do so, the adults would walk on the stalks, but beating the stalks with sticks was more entertaining to us kids. After we had a pile of rice kernels on the ground, some of the ladies would use big flat baskets woven from straw to fan away the last bit of husk. Tiny flakes of rice husk would fill the air. If you were close by, you couldn't help but sneeze!

All the rice would then be placed on a big straw mat to dry in the sun. It was a beautiful thing to see that pile of yellow rice soaking up the sun, knowing that for many months it was going to keep our stomachs full and happy. The next day we were back in the field to do the same thing again. But even after we had stripped the field empty, we weren't done.

After all the rice was dry, then it was time to pound it. To do that, we used a big wooden mortar and pestle. The pestle was a heavy wooden pole about as tall as an adult and about as thick as a man's arm. One end was round to pound rice and the other end was pointed. The mortar was a hollowed-out log about as big around as a small tree and flat on the bottom. It was about as tall as a man's knee so that whatever was inside couldn't bounce out when pounded. We would pound many things: peanuts for paste, dried okra to put in soups, dried shrimp to flavor different foods, and of course, rice.

There was a lot of time and effort put into pounding rice. We had white rice and also brown rice. To get brown rice we only needed to pound on the rice until all the husks were off, then we would fan off the husks leaving only the brown rice kernels; but to get white rice we would continue to pound the brown rice over and over until it became white. It could easily take an hour or more.

I used to enjoy watching the older girls pound the rice. To get the job done faster, two girls would pound together in the same mortar. This produced a very interesting rhythm as they worked. They usually took turns pounding, one would lift her wooden pole while the other brought hers down. They would continue to do this over and over. When there were more than two girls pounding, the whole village would be filled with a thump-thump-thump rhythm. The older girls were so good at pounding that they could throw their poles high in the air, clap their hands, catch their poles on the way down, and still continue with the rhythm. It was very entertaining. The other kids and I would watch them and clap for them as they did their tricks. I remember smiling as I watched, because I knew that someday my turn would come.

I also learned how to plant and harvest peanuts. Growing peanuts was very important to us, because we ate them in so many different ways. We ate them fresh from the ground, dried, roasted, or boiled. We also made peanut paste to use in a variety of food dishes. Growing up, peanuts were one of our main foods. It was hard not to eat them fresh while harvesting them, but eating too many raw peanuts could cause stomachaches! I remember every time I got an upset stomach my grandmother would make me drink a slimy, awful-smelling, bitter-tasting drink to help settle my stomach. It worked, but it also made me poop a lot.

GRANDMOTHER

Let me tell you about my grandmother. I never knew my parents or any of my siblings. My grandmother raised me. I must have been very young when she took me in, because she is the only person I remember being around. I am not really sure what happened to my parents or how I came to be with my grandmother. She once told me that my dad passed away before the war and my mother passed away after him. I was never told how either of them died or anything else about them. It is sad to have parents that you don't even know by name, whose faces you never even saw. But my grandmother was just like a mother to me. She was very tall and skinny and was always smiling. Every time she smiled at me, all I could see were her orange teeth.

Most of the adults in the village, including my

grandmother, chewed cola nuts, which turned their teeth orange. I remember going with her to pick cola. The cola tree was big and had pods hanging on it. From the outside the pods looked like a fruit, but when you cracked them open there were cola nuts inside. I had only had cola nuts once. My grandmother gave me one to try and I remember as soon as I bit into it, I spit it out! The taste was very bitter. Cola nuts were also used as a gift. At the end of the Ramadan fast my grandmother would pick a lot of them, wrap them up in yam leaves, and pass them around.

My grandmother always seemed happy. She went out of her way to take care of other people. I wasn't the only child she was taking care of. Our side of the house was always filled with kids and she always made sure that there was plenty of food for us to eat.

Growing up, I would always work beside her and sleep beside her. I could tell she loved me. She always kept me close to her. I used to love being with her. Everywhere she went, I wanted to go.

I remember one time my grandmother got very sick. I am not sure what was wrong with her. I just remember one of the ladies prepared something for her to drink. It was water with some white powder and an egg cracked into one of our wooden cups. After she drank it, she threw up then went to sleep. The next day the lady gave her the same thing, with the same result. I remember she was weak for a while, but she got better.

Growing up in my village, even though there wasn't any hospital we were always taken care of whenever we were sick, bitten by snakes, or injured. The older people in the village always seemed to know what to do when someone got hurt. There was one time one of the men harvesting the rice cut himself badly. When he was brought back from the field I remember seeing his leg covered in blood. The older ladies began gathering leaves and herbs and pounding them to make a paste for his wound. I remember him lying there, out in the open, yelling as they covered his leg with the medicine. Then they bandaged it with some of the leaves they had gathered. After they were done, he was moved underneath one of the shade trees and he slept for a long time. For days they did the same thing to his leg. After a while he got better and was up and about.

Another incident I remember was when a man was bitten by a snake. This happened at the farm, where we had some grass huts to rest in. He was carried back from the field with sweat pouring down his face. The older men took him into one of the huts. For a long time we could hear him yelling loudly. I don't know what they did to him in there, but when they were finished and came out, most of them had splashes of blood on their clothes. He also slept for very long time and when he woke up he came out walking just fine, with his leg wrapped in leaves.

The rainy season brought a disease that was hard to avoid. It would rain pretty much every day, and we had to walk in dirty water that contained waste from humans, cows, goats, and other animals. Our feet would become infected with some kind of bacteria that turned the webs between our toes white. When that happened, our feet would itch like crazy. I would scratch between my toes, even using a rock or a stick because using my hands wasn't enough. I would scratch until the webs of my toes would bleed.

I remember my grandmother would once again make the white paste medicine and put it between my toes. Then she would have me lie down by the fire with my feet dangling between stakes to dry. It usually took several days to heal and until then we couldn't put our feet on the ground. The best part was that while we were healing someone usually carried us on their back with our feet wrapped in papaya leaves when we would go back and forth to our farm. When we needed to use the restroom, someone would carry us behind a tree. After we did our thing, they would come back to get us.

At a young age, I had to learn how to climb trees to pick mangoes, papayas, and avocados. All the children in the village had to learn to climb trees to stay safe from wild animals. Climbing trees was something we also did for fun. I remember we used to play climbing games to see who could climb fastest to the very top of a tree and pick its fruit. I was never able to win because I am scared of heights. I would climb halfway up then stop to cheer for the other kids, or stay at the bottom and watch for snakes on the trees. If I saw one, I would yell really loudly to warn everyone. Once the winner made it to the top, he or she would shake the tree to cause its fruit to drop. It was very entertaining trying to dodge the falling fruit.

I also used to walk long distances. Every day we had to walk from our village to the farm to work. I remember this part very well because I hated it. I hated having to get up early in the morning and walk barefoot what seemed like miles and miles in the cold to get to the farm before the sun came up. It didn't matter what the weather was like, we still had to walk the distance.

During the rainy season it was awful. We would walk in high water as it still continued to pour down rain. We didn't have any umbrellas and we couldn't wait for the rain to stop.

It was so hard trying to keep up with the adults. I pretty much had to run the whole distance to keep up because my legs were short. It usually didn't take long before tears would start pouring down my face. Once in a while my grandmother would hold my hand and walk with me. She never offered to pick me up, though. How could she when she was already carrying heavy things on her head and in her hands? Because we didn't have any place at the farm to store things, we had to take everything we needed back and forth each day.

There was one part of that marathon walk that I hated the most. Every day we had to go through the dark, cold forest. It was so scary to me that every time we got to it you would not find me in the front or in the back. I had to be in the middle. I was afraid if I was in the front or in the back something would grab me away, so I felt safer being in the middle. Going back to town after a long day of work was not so scary because the moon and stars always lit up the forest. The physical labor in the hot sun was hard, but we lived a pretty good life. We had enough to eat. We never had to go hungry.

Now, let me explain a little bit about the houses in my village. There were not a lot of houses because many family members lived together in the same house. My family had a decent house. It was made out of mud bricks, the floors were made of cement, and it had a tin roof. We didn't have any beds. We slept on handmade mats placed on the floor, which was nice in the heat of the night because the floor cooled us off, but it wasn't so pleasant in the rainy season!

Rainy season brought many unwelcome visitors, such as ants. In the rainy season they would be all over the place, even in our homes and outhouses. There were two types of ants, tiny red ants and big black driver ants. The tiny ants didn't hurt much when they bit, but the big driver ant bites were very painful. They would travel in long lines of millions of ants. We avoided stepping on those lines at all costs! I remember one time we were going to the farm and I accidently stepped on a line of them. I was running with one of the younger girls when we came upon them. We both stepped on them, but I got more ants on me. I remember the pain as they started biting me, but I couldn't move. I just started screaming. My grandmother came to pull me away from them. She took my clothes off and shook the ants out.

Then she pulled off each ant that had stuck its jaws into me. The problem with these ants is that their heads stay attached even when their bodies are pulled off! It was so painful trying to get their heads out of my skin. I spent most of that day in pain from their bites.

I also hated millipedes. The way they moved their many legs was disgusting to me. My grandmother told me to kill them whenever I saw them because they were poisonous, but I couldn't stand to kill them, because they released a strong odor when they were squished. In the rainy season a lot of them would roam around and once in a while we would find a couple of them in our outhouse. Every time that happened, I preferred going behind a tree to going in the outhouse.

I hated to use the outhouse alone at night because other uninvited guests sometimes would appear out of nowhere. I don't know why, but our outhouse always had big ugly lizards climbing on the walls and some of them always managed to be right by the door. But the creatures I feared most were snakes. I was afraid that if I squatted down to go, a snake would come up out of the hole and bite my bottom. I don't know why, but I was more scared of snakes at night than in daylight. At night whenever I got up to use the outhouse I always woke my grandmother to go with me. She was my eyes and ears while I was going. We didn't have electric lights so we usually relied on the moon and the stars at night, but I do remember using a lantern in the outhouse!

Living in a place where there were no electric lights we got to enjoy the beauty of the night. The bright moon and sparkling stars up in the sky were beautiful to see. I never had trouble seeing where I was going at night. There was enough light from the moon and the stars.

Because all the people in my town were Muslims, we had a nice mosque where the adults prayed. I only visited the mosque once, because underage kids weren't allowed in. Each year during the month of Ramadan, all the adults would fast for 28 days. The adults wouldn't eat or drink from sunup until sundown, but we kids were exempt from fasting. In order to finish breakfast before sunup, my grandmother would wake me up very early in the morning before the roosters crowed. I liked the eating part; not so much the getting up part. And as always, as soon as we were finished eating, we would pack everything to take with us to the farm. We still went to the farm during Ramadan, but the adults wouldn't work as hard because of going all day without food and water. In mid-day while they were resting, we kids would play games or sit in the shade eating mangoes, papayas, and peanuts. During the month of Ramadan, we always went home from the fields before the sun went down, that way the adults could go pray at the mosque. After sundown the adults would eat. The month of fasting was always fun for us kids because we got to eat food that we didn't normally eat on a daily basis. There would be special foods just for the month of Ramadan. The ladies made a pudding of rice flour that I especially liked.

Working the farm in the hot sun was hard, but we lived a pretty good life in Mafunta. We kids had fun and plenty to eat. We never had to go hungry. It was a peaceful life. But it didn't stay peaceful.

STRANGE BIRDS

In my village, not a lot of people came in or went out, so most of the time we didn't know what was happening in the outside world. As a child I didn't even know there *was* an outside world. Then one night, we saw bright lights and we heard loud sounds far away. All of us kids were outside playing running games when the lights and sounds began. I remember we stopped playing to look in that direction. We kids were called into the house early that night. The whole village was quiet as we all sat looking in the direction of the lights and sounds. While we were trying to sleep, we kept on hearing the sounds.

For several days, we wondered what was going on because we kept hearing the same loud sounds, and we kept seeing the same bright lights at night. Every day and night the sounds and lights kept getting closer and closer to us. For a while the adults instructed us to stay close to the house, but no one knew what was going on. Eventually we became accustomed to the lights and sounds and we went on with our lives.

As a child growing up in a village, there was one thing I and the other children always looked forward to, seeing the big white bird high in the sky. In the village we called anything that flew a bird. We did not know where it was coming from or where it was going or what to call it, but I remember that anytime we heard it we would stop whatever we were doing and wave to it with excitement. Even some of the adults would join us. As a child, I remember always looking forward to seeing that big white bird in the sky. I have now come to know that big white bird as an airplane. It was a treat when more than one went by in a day. Little did I know then that those birds that brought me so much joy were also going to destroy my world.

I very well remember the night it happened. As usual, all of us kids were outside playing, chasing each other, having fun, and enjoying the night. The whole village was full of light from the moon and the stars. But that night a different kind of bird came to visit my village. I now know this kind is called a helicopter. We were so excited because there were more than one, and the sounds that they made were much louder than the other birds that passed over our farm. That night they were so low above us that they made dust rise up from the ground, and their lights lit up the village. We were excited because we had never seen anything like them before; and as always, young and old, we all ran to wave to them.

Then it happened.

I heard a noise so loud it made my ears ring. It was like the loud sounds we had been hearing previously, except this time it was much louder. Bright lights and dark smoke and dust came with the sound. There was a new sound too, a smaller fast-repeating sound that seemed to go on and on. Every time I heard this fast sound, puffs of dust would rise up from the ground. I didn't know this sound was from a machine gun on the helicopter. I had never known gunfire before. I remember the dust was so thick it was choking me. It was hard to breathe or see where I was running. Everywhere we ran, bright lights on the birds seemed to follow us. We didn't know where to go!

The whole village went crazy. Everyone was running and calling for their family members, not knowing what to do or where to find safety. Young and old were running over each other. There was so much chaos and the dust was so thick that everywhere I ran I was bumping into someone or trampling over a body on the ground.

After a while, most people started running toward their houses. Everywhere we ran, people were falling and some were not getting up. I started running toward my house, but didn't get far before I tripped and fell on the ground. I remember people stumbling over me. Every time I tried to get up somebody would knock me back down. I called for help, but no one could hear me due to the noise and chaos.

For a while it felt like I was going to be trampled to death. I could feel the weight of each person as he ran over me. When the chaos started to die down, I lay there for a while before I was able to get up. As soon as I got to my feet, I started running toward the forest like everyone else.

I remember just running and running, not knowing where to go, who to follow, or who to call. I was just running as fast as my little kid legs could go. For a while I was running with a bunch of other people, then one of the big birds began following us and everybody scattered.

I ran for a long, long time. I didn't know when I should stop, so I kept running and running. As I was running, I could feel pain from being cut as I ran barefoot through the bush over rocks and thorns. Eventually I wasn't able to see where I was going in the dark forest, so I stopped.

That night I was so confused. I didn't know where

anybody was or what to do. I didn't know where my grandmother was or how to go about looking for her. I was alone, scared, and cold. I wasn't sure if I should sleep. I tried to stay awake but couldn't, so I dozed off hoping I was not sleeping with a snake or a wild animal.

When morning came, everyone came out of their hiding places one by one. It turned out there were other people hiding around me. Everyone had been so quiet that I had thought I was all alone. Parents were calling for their children and their family members. Everyone looked confused and scared like I was. We were not prepared for this. There was no plan for what to do. I wasn't sure what I was supposed to do or how I should feel. I remember just standing there in the midst of everyone calling for their loved ones, then I heard my name and there was my grandmother running toward me!

Once she found me, she started calling out for the other children, but there were only a couple of us that came. I remember her crying as she gathered us together and we all walked hand-in-hand away from our village toward the farm. That awful night was the very moment the war came to us and it changed everything for us. I never saw my village again after that night.

Our farm became our new home. The big birds became something we feared and hid from every time. I remember my grandmother telling me to always find a bush and hide underneath it until the big bird was gone. From that day on, every time we saw one everyone, young and old, would run around trying to find a bush to hide under.

Nothing was the same. Everyone was on edge all the time. During the day we had to stay quiet and close to the farm. We had to stay alert, watching for the big birds, and running for safety if we saw one. At night, we weren't allowed to make fire. We did all our cooking during the day and put out the fire before dark so our hiding place would not be discovered. Even though the temperature was 90 degrees or higher each day, it got cold in the middle of the night and early morning. Normally we would have slept with a fire all night for warmth. With no fire, we had to sleep close to each other to keep warm. During the rainy season we stayed up all night, cold and wet.

As the days went by, more people started coming to our farm. Some of them were crying and calling out names of family members that they had left behind. They were sweaty and dirty and some were covered with blood. Hungry babies were crying as their mamas carried them on their backs. As a little kid I didn't know what was going on, but I could tell that the newcomers were very afraid and so were the adults from my village. The rules of staying quiet and close to the farm got stricter and we were punished if we made too much noise or went too far. Even with the extra people on our farm, we still had plenty of food to eat. We were fortunate to live on a farm that provided a lot of food for us. We had big ponds for fishing. We had mangoes, papayas, oranges, and coconuts to eat. The forest near the farm also had animals for the men to hunt, but we children were instructed never to enter the forest.

For a while nothing happened, but still we lived our lives scared and keeping watch for the big bird in the sky. One day, though, around midafternoon when we were cooking our food, I heard the same fast and loud sound that I had heard coming from the birds before, and like before, we all went crazy trying to escape. But this time it was different. There weren't any birds. This time we heard voices yelling at us not to move. But, scared as we were, we did the opposite and ran toward the forest. Running into the forest was scary, but not as scary as the people chasing us.

Once again, we weren't ready for them. We did not see them coming. I remember suddenly hearing the fast loud sound and then people screaming. And again, we had to leave everything behind. Even though this time we had stored food away to take with us, there was not enough time to get it or to do anything but run.

Our next camping place was not so nice. It wasn't like the farm. It was more out in the open, but there were still some trees around for us to hide behind if needed. Everything was all dirt and dry. We slept on hard rocky ground every night, whereas at our farm we'd had handmade mats to sleep on.

Sleeping on the ground during rainy season without a mat was awful. When the ground became soaked with rain, earthworms would come out and crawl on me. If not earthworms, then ants or other insects. And sleeping on the wet ground made me very cold. I was miserable at night during rainy season at that camp.

Food was limited at this new camp. There were no fishing ponds, fruit trees, or fields. We started eating only one meal a day, usually just before we went to bed. I'm not sure how, but the adults dug a hole to collect water. It wasn't clean and didn't taste good, but we used it for drinking and cooking.

While we were staying at this camp, we ate a lot of berries. I remember following my grandmother as she picked them. We also ate a lot of termites. During the rainy season, many of them flew around. Catching them was a thrill for us kids. The best time to catch them was very early in the morning when the sky was still foggy. In the rainy season we also found big white larvae in rotting trees. We ate them alive and also fried. It took a while to get used to eating them, especially the live ones, but we needed food and they were easy to find.

Every few days the big white birds would fly over and we would hide. But they passed over and didn't bother us. Every night we listened for helicopters, but they never came back.

For a long time, nothing changed. Then one day we saw a big, loud truck coming toward us. I had never seen a car or truck before. When we saw it coming, we ran and hid close by, expecting to hear the loud fast sound, but we didn't. It had become our habit to run whenever we saw or heard anything unusual, but we wouldn't run far from the camp so we would know when to come back. From my hiding place, I saw a man came out of the truck. When my grandmother came out and started talking to him, we knew it was safe to come out from our hiding. It turned out the driver was her son-in-law.

It was years before I learned this, but my grandmother had a daughter who lived in Freetown, the capital of Sierra Leone. I've been told that Freetown had been a well-developed city before the war. There were paved roads, a few people owned cars, and there were taxis and trucks. My grandmother's daughter's husband was a truck driver there. I don't know how, but somehow he was able to find our campsite. He explained to my grandmother that there had been fighting in Freetown but it was calmer there now. He had come to take her and anyone else who wanted to go back to Freetown in the truck.

That was a happy day for all of us. Even though I didn't know what he was talking about, I knew I was ready to get out of that place. It was no fun having to sleep on bare ground in shelters made of sticks and leaves through the cold nights and having to get up every morning soaking wet during the rainy season. I was tired of having to run every time we heard something and having to go to bed hungry. I didn't know what Freetown was, but I knew I wanted to go with him.

After he was finished explaining it to my grandmother, all of us kids and some of the adult moms with infants were lined up. I was close to the back of the line. One by one people were lifted up into the truck. As the line got shorter, the truck got fuller. Every time someone was lifted up into the truck I would lean forward to see if there was still room for me. Finally it was my turn and I was happy that there was still room left! I stepped forward and raised my hands to be lifted up, but somebody pulled me back. I looked up and it was my grandmother standing over me. As I said before, my grandmother was a very tall lady. She got on her knees, eye level with me, and said, "No, Fatu. Stay with Grandmother."

I started crying and yelling "No! No!" over and over, but she wrapped her arms around me and held me tight. I fought hard, trying to free myself from her strong grip, but it was no use. She held me until the truck pulled away. As soon as she released me from her grip, I ran and ran to catch up with the truck, but the faster I ran, the farther away it got. I finally gave up chasing it. I stood there crying and hoping it would come back. But it didn't.

After a long while, I walked back to the campsite. My grandmother was getting ready to cook the little food we still had left. As I sat down on the ground she knelt down to me and said, "Grandmother needs Fatu." I started crying again saying "No!" over and over again. I couldn't understand why she wanted me to stay. Why did she let all the other kids go in the truck but make me stay? That day all the kids were gone except for me. It seemed unfair to me that I was the only kid left with the rest of the adults. There were only a few people left in the camp now. Once I finally calmed myself down, I started helping her with the cooking.

Later that day before we were even done with the cooking, I heard again the same loud fast sound and the rebels screaming at us not to move. Once again, none of us saw them coming and nobody was prepared for anything except to run. My grandmother started yelling my name. I answered in a shaky voice "I am here, Grandmother." She grabbed my hand and we started running together.

Let me explain what it feels like to be running for your life. In the village, running games had been fun for us kids. But running for your life is not fun at all. In fact, there is nothing scarier on this planet than having to run for your life. I remember each time I ran I could feel my heart pounding out of my chest. I could feel sweat pouring down my face and pain in my feet as I ran through everything in my way. There was never time to stop and catch my breath. I had to keep on moving and hope I wouldn't be caught. I had to run fast to survive.

Running without any of your family members is the scariest. It happened to me twice. The first time was the day the birds came to my village, and the second was when the rebels discovered our farm. Both times, I was separated from my grandmother just for a little while. I remember how scared I was, thinking I would never see her again.

Let me get back to the story.

My grandmother grabbed my hand and started pulling me along. I was doing a pretty good job running with her until my curiosity got the best of me. I decided to look back to see what was going on. I wanted to see the people we were running away from. I wanted to see what was so scary about them to make us run away. While I was looking back, a lady in front of us fell. My grandmother went around her but I ended up tripping over her raised leg and landed on top of her. My grandmother came back for me and grabbed my hand to pull me up, but by the time I got to my feet, it was too late. All three of us were captured. The rebels had captured other people as well.

They made us walk back to the campsite, with their pointy sticks at the back of our heads. I know now that those sticks were guns. But I didn't know about guns then. I had never seen a gun. One of the rebel soldiers kept pushing us and yelling at us to move faster.

When we got to the campsite, we were ordered to sit down. My grandmother was still holding on to my hand. We sat on the ground and she wrapped her arms around me. I remember that day not feeling anything. I wasn't sad or afraid. I just sat there leaning against her watching the soldiers, dripping with sweat, pointing their guns at each person that they had lined up. Every time I heard the loud gun sound somebody would fall over and not get back up.

I knew all those people and I watched as each one of them tumbled down. The sound from the guns made me jump out of my skin every time. When they were finished, the ground was covered with bodies and blood. One of the rebels came over where we were sitting, pulled my grandmother up, and told her to go gather food for them. I got up to follow her, but he ordered me to sit back down. After my grandmother left, the lady who'd been captured with us was the only one left alive with me except for the rebels.

I need to explain something before I go on. In this war, the rebels tried every way to make everyone afraid of them. They would burn people alive, rape women and girls, and do many other things that I don't want to talk about. But one of the worst things they did was cut off people's hands or feet. Nearly all the people cut in this way bled to death. But if they survived, everyone who saw them would know how cruel the rebels were. That's why the rebels cut people, so people would be afraid of them. But I didn't know any of that then. On with the story.

After my grandmother left, one of the rebel soldiers pulled out a big machete knife and told the lady who was captured with me to place her hand on one of the wooden logs we used to sit on. She did. He raised the knife high above her hand, but when he was bringing it down to cut her hand off, she pulled away. She was told to place it on the log again. The knife went up and again when it was coming down she pulled away. A third time she was told to place it on the log. The knife went up and when it was coming down she pulled away yet again. By that time, the soldier was very angry. Once more her hand was placed on the log. The soldier lifted the knife, but this time as he was bringing it down, he moved the knife and cut the back of her neck instead. I watched as she tumbled forward face down onto the ground.

For a while, as she lay there dying, the back of her

neck was just white. Then blood started coming. By then, I was terrified, looking at all those dead people around me. I didn't know what to do or how I should feel. I just sat there hoping my grandmother would come back. She had been gone for a long time and she was still not back. I was looking at the direction she went when I heard the soldier with the knife shout "You!"

Let me tell you how it feels to watch not one, not two, but several people being killed right in front of you. I was just a small child. I couldn't understand what I was seeing. There weren't really any clear thoughts or feelings. My emotions were all mixed up. I remember being scared, but it wasn't because I understood what had just happened. I was scared mostly because my grandmother wasn't there. But now, as an adult writing about that horrific day, I can tell you, it is a nightmare to replay the death scene of a person in your memory, to see people that you knew, people who used to talk with you, laugh with you, and live with you lying on the ground dead. It is a terrifying image that stays with you forever.

Now, where were we? Oh, yes. I was looking in the direction that my grandmother went when I heard "You!"

The soldier with the knife walked up to me and told me to do the same thing, to place my right hand on the log. I did what he said. He raised the knife, but as he brought it down I pulled away with fear. The machete hit the log so hard that one side of the log split open. Again he put my hand on the log and lifted the knife. I remember that very moment. I was sitting on the ground with my hand on the log, my heart pounding out of my chest and sweat pouring down my forehead. I was confused and scared, but I remembered what happened to the other lady. I was too scared to pull my hand back again.

He brought the knife down hard.

Thump!

The knife cut right through my wrist and into the log. It happened so fast. I felt a little flash of light on my face, and the heat from the knife as it hit my skin. Just one hit and my hand went flying off.

For a while, I didn't feel anything. No pain. Not anything. I couldn't even make a sound. It was like my mouth was glued shut. I couldn't yell or move. I just sat there looking at my hand flopping like a fish trying to get back into the water. I don't understand how a cut-off hand could do that, but that's what I remember. It went on for a long time. Meanwhile, blood was squirting out of my stump like crazy. It didn't take long before I was covered in blood.

After the soldiers were done with me, they took nearly everything in the camp and left. I was sitting there alone, covered in blood not knowing what to do or how I should feel. It was a long time before I looked at my stump, and what I saw was blood, a bone, and a little bit of twitching flesh hanging out. As I was looking at my stump, I remember feeling nothing. No crying. No tears. I just sat there alone looking at the mess at the end of my arm.

After a while, I started getting cold even though it was a hot day. My body was shivering. My teeth were chattering. Even though the sun was hot, I couldn't keep my body from shaking. The wind felt cold as it blew through my wet dress and my uncovered wound. I became very thirsty and my mouth and throat went dry. When my hand was chopped off, I remember another odd feeling. My body didn't feel like it was mine. I felt like I was in somebody else's body that I couldn't control.

I sat there covered in my own blood until the sun started to go down. I knew it would soon be dark. After many tries, I was able to get up on my feet and I started walking in the direction that my grandmother had gone. I called out to her but she didn't answer. I knew I needed to find someone to help me. After all, I was just a little kid. I think I must have been six or seven years old.

Two other ladies had been hiding close by the campsite and came out when they heard me calling. But when they looked at me I saw fear in their eyes.

Even though they knew me well, they didn't know what to do with me. They quickly gathered up some of the little things the rebels had left behind and started walking down the same path that my grandmother and I were on when we were captured. I tried to follow them, but I was too weak and dizzy. Every step I took landed me on the ground but they just kept on walking. Finally I lost sight of them, and once again it was just me and the dead people. It was getting too dark to walk anyway.

I walked the few steps back to where I was sitting before. Hunger came to me. I could hear my stomach growling and feel it twisting. My mouth and throat were so dry. After a while, the wind started blowing hard and things were flying everywhere. My stump was soon covered with dust and leaves. Next thing I knew, it began to rain! Strange that rain came that day, because it wasn't even rainy season. I was able to find a wooden cup to capture some rain water and boy, did I drink!! My body was craving water more than it was craving food.

The rain went on for a long time. Suddenly, I started to feel pain. It was so unbearable at first that it made me sick to my stomach. Moving my stump made the pain even worse. That night, even though I was very tired, I had a hard time falling asleep. There wasn't any place dry for me to go to get warm. I was soaking wet, cold, and in pain.

The pain was so intense that it drove me crazy throughout the night. I was in so much pain that night, all I wanted to do was die. Through all that, somehow I was able to fall asleep, because the next day I woke to find myself with the rest of the bodies in a puddle of bloody rainwater. The pain was still screaming at me. Again, the first thing that I wanted was water to drink. I was so weak that getting up from the ground was a struggle. Every attempt landed me in the puddle again.

Once I was up, I looked at my hand and I noticed the skin where I was cut was pulling back now, and more flesh was hanging out. It was still oozing blood. With baby steps, I was able to walk to the water hole near the camp. It took me a while to get there because I was so dizzy. My thirst was so strong that I placed my face right into the water and drank and drank and drank. I drank so much that it made my stomach hurt.

I realized my grandmother wasn't coming back, and I knew I needed to look for help. I started walking in the same direction she and I had been running when we'd been caught. As I was walking, I saw vultures already eating the dead people. Some were flying over me waiting for me to collapse too, which I did many times, but I always managed to get back up before they started eating me. It took me a while to walk anywhere because I was so dizzy.

WALKING

Despite my baby steps and frequent falls, I eventually came into a big open field. Tall dry grass was all around me. It was really hard to walk in that grass. Every step left me with a cut, but after a while I was in the middle of the field. Suddenly the biggest snake I had ever seen in my life slithered past me, parting the grass as it went. I just stood there in the blazing sun, dripping with sweat and about to pass out, waiting for that snake to go by. Once it was gone, I went in the opposite direction!

It took me a while, but I finally made it into the cool forest. There I was able to find drinking water in tree leaves to drink, since it had rained the night before. I was also able to find fruit to eat. When it got too dark to walk, I picked a tree to lie under. At this point, I didn't care about trying to hide from wild animals. As weak as I was, climbing a tree with only one hand was out of the question, as were running away or defending myself with a stick. I was helpless. Yet, during all the days and nights I spent in the forest alone, not once did I ever come in contact with a wild animal. I had no shoes and yet not once did I step on any poisonous creature. I walked for maybe one week or more in that forest. I wasn't sure which way to go. There wasn't any path. I had to make my own. As I walked, all I could see were tall trees, hanging vines, and thorn bushes.

One time I found myself caught in the middle of a thorn bush. I stepped right into it without seeing it and the more I panicked due to the pain, the more it kept poking every inch of my body. I was bleeding at different places trying to pull each thorn off me. My stump bled the most, because every time I pulled a thorn out of it some flesh would tear away. By that time, my stump and much of the rest of my body was covered with a mixture of blood and dirt. I was stuck in that bush for a while. Every time I moved around to pull a thorn out, another would stick in me. When I bent down to pull out the thorns on my legs, my hair or my bottom would get caught. It was a painful and exhausting mess. Even now I am reminded of that day when I look at the scars on my body.

Eventually I freed myself and I started walking again because I wanted to get out of that creepy forest. Some parts of the forest were dark and cold because big trees blocked the sun. I kept finding water in tree leaves and was able to find food to eat. I was no longer as weak as I was before, so I was able to walk a little bit faster.

After several days, I knew I was coming to the edge of the forest because I could see light ahead of me. I came to a dirt road that I had to cross, but it was at the bottom of a deep ditch cut through a hill, with a steep dirt bank on either side. Just as I was about to step out of the trees, some big trucks filled with people came around a curve heading in my direction. A lot of the people in the trucks were carrying guns. When I saw the first truck, I stepped back into the forest and hid. One by one, I saw the trucks pass. I stayed low until I couldn't hear them anymore, then got up and started to cross again.

Crossing to the other side was not easy. I didn't realize how soft the dirt on the bank was until I tried to walk down it. I lost my footing and tumbled all the way down, covering my stump in dirt, leaves, and small sticks. When I reached the bottom, I looked up and down the road to make sure there weren't any more trucks. It was then that I recognized the road. It was the road that led from my village to our farm! I remembered in the evenings when we were walking home from our farm we would meet other families at the very spot I was standing. We would then walk back to the village together. In the mornings we would all walk from the village together until we got to that spot, then we would turn onto a path while they walked further down that road. Knowing those trucks were heading toward my old village, I was afraid to walk on the road in either direction. I decided to cross to the other side and keep walking through the bush. I knew I needed to find some people soon to help me. My stump was getting worse and there was nothing I could do for myself.

Climbing up the other side of the road bank was a struggle. Every time I grabbed onto a bush or a vine it would break loose. I had to walk to different spots just to find something sturdy to pull myself up. Even then, I had trouble with only one hand. It was a good thing that those trucks went by before I started crossing, because there was no way I could have made it down the first side and up the other quickly without being noticed. Who knows what they would have done to me?

Once I made it up to the top, I walked for a little while before coming to a lake that I had to cross. I didn't realize how deep the lake was until I stepped in. As soon as I did, I started sinking. I tried to grab anything to keep myself up, but nothing was in sight. I just kept sinking. I can't tell you exactly how I managed to get out of that lake, but somehow I did.

After all that, I looked again at my stump. It kept looking worse. Not only was it dirty, but now there was pus coming out of it. The pain was no longer as intense as before. Once again I started walking, and in the far distance I could see smoke. As I got closer, I could hear people talking but as soon as they saw me coming, they started running away. When I reached their campsite they stopped running and just looked at me, not knowing what to do.

One family was kind enough to take me in. They washed my stump and used a cloth to wrap it. When they were wrapping my stump, there is no word to express how painful it was. I guess my stump had become so sensitive that even a little bit of pressure was enough to drive me crazy. The cloth was so tight it made my stump throb with pain. For the first time since I'd lost my hand, I cried.

After that was all done, they gave me food and water, but I was in too much pain to eat or drink. I just sat and cried until night came and everyone went into their little huts to sleep. They left me outside because my stump was starting to smell. During the night, the pain was so unbearable that the only way to cope was to walk around all night long, holding my arm up in the air.

Morning finally came but even then I wasn't able

to sleep. I watched as everyone went about their lives. Kids my age were playing and having fun. Parents were gathering food. But I was too weak to do any of that. The smell of my stump was attracting a lot of vultures. They started walking close to me, watching for me to die. Another day went by with me in torment, followed by another sleepless night. Day after day and night after night, my agony continued.

After a few days, my bandage was soaking wet and started leaking. My arm started feeling heavier and bigger. My smell was getting worse too, and not just from my stump. I wasn't taking a bath. Also, I was unable to give myself proper hygiene after using the restroom. We didn't use toilet paper to clean ourselves, we used water. This involves using both hands to complete the task. With only one hand, I couldn't clean myself well.

Someone finally remembered me and came to help change my dressing. When he took the bandage off, an awful thing happened. Maggots came spilling out. There were so many that my stump was covered with them. All I could see as the cloth was being unwrapped were white squirming maggots. They started going everywhere on my body and on the ground. And the smell! It was so unbearable that the guy who was helping me had to cover his nose and it made me vomit all over my shirt.

In order to kill the maggots, he had me dip my

stump in hot water over and over again. There is no word to describe the pain from that. When no more maggots came out, he wrapped my stump again.

I was still alive, but I was getting weaker, skinnier, dirtier, and smellier. The smell got so bad that they moved me under a mango tree far from the campsite. Vultures were always watching me and walking close to me. Day after day and night after night, I sat underneath that tree. I was scared sitting there by myself during the cold dark nights.

I can't imagine how bad I looked. My face was covered with my own dried tears and dried snot. Flies put me through agony, biting at my wounds every chance they got. The vultures started getting closer to me. It was like they could sense life was leaving me. I could feel it too. I was so weak I couldn't even scare away the flies. Getting up to use the bathroom became too much of a struggle. I had to sit in my own waste.

Once in a while, somebody would remember me and offer me food and water to drink, but I was so weak that even putting food in my mouth seemed too difficult to do. Sometimes somebody else would help me with my dressing. Every time, as soon as the dressing was opened, crawling, squirming maggots spilled out and they had me plunge my stump in hot water to get rid of them. But the pain from the hot water wasn't as intense as it had been the first few times they changed my bandage. My hand was rotting away every day and so was my life. I was so miserable and in so much pain that all I wanted to do was die. In fact, I think I did almost die, because I really can't explain what happened next.

FREETOWN

The next thing I remember is waking up in a Doctors Without Borders clinic in Freetown. I really don't know how I got there or remember anything about my surgery. I just woke up in a place I'd never been with my stump covered with white bandages. I was scared and confused, which got worse when I was greeted by a tall man with white skin, white hair, and a white beard saying something that I couldn't understand. I had never seen anyone like him before and when he came closer to my bed, the only thing I could do was lie there and cry because I was so scared of him.

After a couple days of lying in bed, one of the nurses took me for a walk around the clinic. That's when I was able to see it all. People were lying there with no leg or no arm, or no legs or arms. The whole place was nothing but sadness. New people were being brought in every day, and people young and old were dying every day. While I was at the clinic, no one I knew came to visit me. The only person that came to see me was the tall, white-bearded, white-haired, white man to talk with me, even though I couldn't understand what he was saying. In fact, I couldn't understand anybody, not even the local people, because I spoke a different language from them.

I remember the first time I saw my stump without any bandages. It still had the stitches in it. I was surprised at how short my arm was. During the operation they had to remove more of my arm because so much of it was rotten. When the solider cut me, he only took my hand off. I still had my forearm down to the wrist. After the surgery, only a little bit below the elbow was left. I thought it was very ugly.

While I was living in the clinic, I remember every day there would be flies swarming the place. There would be people sitting outside with a bandaged hand or foot and flies would swarm around them. There was a really strong odor, too. Every day I watched as people scared vultures away from the sick people lying on mats outside. Skinny, hungry dogs roamed around looking for anything to eat. I saw dead people being carried away pretty much every day.

After being in the clinic a while, I started looking more like a human being. Before, I was so skinny and malnourished that you could count every bone in my body. I started gaining strength and my stump was healing. Soon, it was time for me to leave the clinic to make room for others. There was a special camp in Freetown for people who had fled their homes because of the war and had lost arms or legs. Their family members could stay there too. That's where the people at the clinic decided to take me.

The day I arrived in the amputee camp, the government truck came. It came once a month to give out food to all the wounded refugees and their families. Every time the truck came, somebody would read each wounded person's name out loud, and they would ask how many people were in the household. That way they could give out the correct amount of food to last that family for a few weeks. One by one, they started calling out names. When they called mine, I started making my way up through the crowd when suddenly somebody stepped right in front of me. I looked up, and there was my grandmother!

Tears were streaming down her face, then she knelt down and took my stump in her hands and cried even harder. The joy I felt when I saw her, words can't even express. After crying and hugging, we went up to the truck to collect our food. Then we went to a building to sign me up for a room at the camp. Once again my grandmother and I were together. That night, she told me that she had been coming to the camp and the clinic nearly every day looking for me.

I never did get the story of how either of us managed to get to Freetown. I did learn, though, that the reason we were able to hear the loud sounds and see the bright lights in the beginning is because Mafunta was only 45 kilometers from Freetown. The sounds and lights were explosions from fighting in villages between our village and Freetown. We were that close to the war and yet we didn't know anything about it until the night it came to us.

Staying at the camp wasn't easy. We had food, but sometimes it wasn't enough and sleeping space was tight. My grandmother decided to take in other kids. To have money to buy food and other necessary things, I became a beggar.

Every morning, I would go out and walk the streets of Freetown with other amputees, asking people for money. Sometimes people would give me money, other times they would give me rice, beans, peanuts, or dried fish, just anything to help out. It was very hard doing that every day in the hot sun or pouring rain, walking barefoot up and down the streets all day long. There were times when I would beg all day and still not have anything to take home, because there were many other people begging too.

It took me a while to get used to doing things with just one hand. If my grandmother was around she would do everything for me. She would always help me with my bathing. She would help me put on my clothes and take them off and cleaned me after I used the toilet. I can't imagine what my life in the camp would have been like if she hadn't been around. I saw many kids who didn't have anyone helping them. They were so hungry they would steal food to survive.

Even though the fighting had left Freetown, the camp was not a good place to live. A terrible thing happened to my grandmother one night when she went out to use the restroom. Someone attacked her and left her half naked, lying in some bushes. The next day, she was found by a bunch of kids playing around that area. When she was brought back, I remember looking at her face and all I could see was fear and sadness. My grandmother had always seemed so strong to me, but that day she looked like a scared little girl.

My grandmother was a very devoted Muslim. She prayed several times every day and she usually took a long time doing it. I remember before she prayed she would wash her face, the back of her ears, the back of her neck, her upper arms, and her feet. I used to watch her and follow everything she did. If she washed her face, I would wash my face, and so on. When she started to pray I would also pray with her. I could never sit through the whole prayer though. It took too long and I didn't know the Arabic words.

Every time I got up to leave, her eyes would be open and her mouth moving. I always wondered who she was talking to.

After a couple of years living in the camp, someone decided to help the refugee kids by providing school for us, so I stopped begging and started going to school. I didn't get much out of it though, because I couldn't understand what was going on. The teachers were speaking a language that the other kids knew, but I was just lost and confused. I don't know what happened, but soon we kids from the camp couldn't go to that school anymore, and I was back on the street begging.

More people started showing up at the camp taking pictures and videos, especially of us amputees. I was really camera shy, mostly because I was scared of those white people coming up to me trying to shake my hand. I didn't understand shaking hands because we didn't shake hands in the village. The white people always smiled at me, which I found even scarier. I cried a lot while I was at the camp, not because of hunger or pain, but because of being face-to-face with white people. After a while, I learned how to avoid them. I would run in the other direction every time I saw one.

Life continued. I was getting up early every morning to beg. The government truck was coming once in a while to give us food. Other people would also come to the camp to give out clothes and other things. Sometimes they had to leave because people would fight over the things they were passing out. Life in the camp showed me what war does to people. It makes them crazy. The war left people with so little that the only way to get anything is to overpower someone else to get it. In the village people took care of each other, but in that camp I saw kids fighting with other kids over a bowl of rice just to get food in their bellies. Adults would wrestle with each other on the ground for one pair of pants or a T-shirt. War takes everything from people, even their humanity.

AMERICA

My grandmother was approached one day about the possibility of me coming to America to get a prosthesis. I was with her when she was being told about it. I didn't know what America was, but I remembered that the word sounded nice. Not long after that, my grandmother sat me down and explained to me that I was going somewhere to get a hand. I was very excited at the idea of having two hands again.

Some days later, I was in a taxi cab heading to the Freetown airport. The ride was not pleasant for me. It was my first time being in a car, and with the heat and emotion I was carsick all the way to the airport. Before we got to the airport, I had no idea what was going to happen, so I wasn't prepared. My grand-mother had not explained everything to me, so I wasn't ready.

The first thing I saw at the airport was the big white birds. More than one was there. I started to panic and I started looking around to see what the other people were doing, but everybody else was calm. In fact people were going into the birds and coming out of them. I couldn't understand why nobody was running. I wanted to run and hide but there wasn't anywhere to go, so I stayed very close to my grandmother just in case.

Once inside the airport, I met the other amputees who were leaving. Some of them had been in the camp with me. There were six amputee kids and four adults (two of them were amputees, too).

Even after we had been at the airport for a while, I still didn't know what was about to happen. It was not until I saw the other kids and adults boarding that I realized I too would be going inside one of the big white birds. I started crying and grabbing my grand-mother very tightly, begging her not to make me go. She tried to calm me down but I was so scared that it took a while. Only then did she explain to me that I would be going to America without her. The idea that I would be going without her had never crossed my mind! But now it was clear and I was scared. I couldn't imagine life without her again.

After we shared our good-bye hug, I climbed aboard the plane, crying, with my heart jumping out of my chest. I cried even more when we started to leave the ground. I remember feeling sick to my stomach. My head was dizzy and my palm was sweating. I thought I was going to die. I had never experienced anything like that before, but after being up in the air for a while I got used to it.

We were flying for a while when a lady started giving out snacks and drinks. She came to my row of seats and said something I couldn't understand. The guy that was sitting next to me said something back and pointed, and the lady gave him what he was pointing at. Then she looked at me and smiled and said something, so I pointed too, to a shiny can of what I now know as Sprite.

When she opened the can, it made a sound I had never heard before. I watched as she poured the clear liquid, which I thought was water, into a cup and handed it to me. The man next to me helped me with my tray, then she placed that shiny can on it and left. I took a big drink of this "water," but the taste and feeling as it was going down my throat made me realize it was not water at all! I didn't like the way it made my throat feel while I was drinking, but I do remember thinking "This is really sweet!" So I kept on drinking and drinking and by the time she came back I had already emptied my can.

As she was passing through I pointed again, so she handed me another can. I wasn't even halfway through it when I suddenly burped so loudly that everyone who was sitting near me looked in my direction, laughing. But it wasn't funny to me. I couldn't understand why my chest, throat, and nose were hurting. I couldn't control my tears because the burp made my eyes sting so badly. So for a while, I just sat there and cried my eyes out.

Soon after that, I had to pee. I didn't know what to do or what to say, so I started squirming in my seat. The man next to me noticed, and said something to the lady while pointing at me. He helped me with my tray while she motioned for me to get out. Then one of the ladies in our group took me into a little room. She pointed at the toilet and explained to me what I needed to do. I was able to understand her because she spoke Krio, a language I had learned in Freetown.

Of course, I didn't pay attention to everything she was saying because my pee-dancing was getting intense. She closed the door and left me in the room alone. Even though she had explained what to do, I wasn't sure how to go about doing it. I walked over and looked at the toilet. Every toilet I had ever seen before was just a small hole in the ground for me to squat over. This hole seemed too big. I was afraid if I sat on it I would fall in!

Sitting seemed too risky. I decided to just stand really close above it then pee. That did not go too well! I peed all over myself. It didn't help that the plane kept on moving up and down. When the lady from our group came back to check up on me, I had already taken off my wet pants and was holding them. We looked at each other, then she left and came back with another outfit for me to wear.

Not long after I got back to my seat, the lady that had given me the Sprite started passing out food. I am not sure what I ate, but it was definitely something that I had never eaten before. The taste was very different from what I was used to. But I ate every bite because I was hungry and it was good.

After that, it was time to sleep. Everything got dark. The man next to me got me a pillow and a blanket and helped me with my seat. I am not sure what he did, but it felt comfortable when he was finished. I must have slept for a very long time because when I woke up the ride was over. We had to get off.

I'm not sure where we landed, but I remember being amazed by all the people. There were so many and everyone was moving so fast and loud noises were everywhere, noises that I had never heard before. I couldn't help being jumpy.

We waited for a while then we had to get on another airplane. This time I wasn't scared of getting on. My fear didn't start until I realized that white people were going to be riding with us. There were a lot of them and I even had to sit next to one of them. I didn't cry but I was definitely afraid. This ride wasn't as long as the first one and then we had to get off again. When we got off it was the same thing, a lot of people and a lot of noises, but this time there were people waiting for us. After a brief introduction that I did not understand, we got in a car and drove someplace.

So far you have read about the life that I had before the war, during the war, and at the camp. Next, let me share with you what has happened to me since, how I came to the Land of Freedom, and how I became known as Fatu Litsey. Sit tight! This is a life-changing story. Let's get back to it.

We landed somewhere, we met some people, they introduced themselves, we got in a car and drove off. During the ride I was amazed by all the things that were happening around me. The lights, the buildings, the noises, the people, and the cars were all so new and exciting. Everything was so big and overwhelming. We kids couldn't help it but say things like "Whoa! Wow! What was that?" In Krio, of course.

We came into the United States in September of 2000. When we first came, we landed in Washington, D.C. Our first week in the states, some of us kids were placed with families from Sierra Leone. I believe the main reason we were placed in these homes was to help us a little bit with the culture shock. I remember the family that took me. When I went into their house it had the familiar aroma of African food. That smell gave me a lot of peace.

That day I was introduced to many new things. I remember my shower introduction. The lady said some words I couldn't understand, pulled on something, and before I knew it water was coming down! I remember standing there with my mouth open wondering to myself "Where is that water coming from?" I thought the shower head was able to somehow produce the water, and it scared me to think of that. It was a long time before I was comfortable around a shower head. The first time I took a shower, I remember the stinging feeling as the water hit my skin. It was kind of funny, because growing up in Africa, we have rainy season where it would rain hard nearly every day. As kids, we would run around in the rain but it never stung my skin like the shower did.

Next was the toilet. She explained it, but again, I couldn't understand what she was saying. Then she pushed the handle and a lot of water came rushing in. I didn't like the loud sound it made. It was a while before I got comfortable using a flush toilet. For a while, I was still afraid to sit down, thinking I might fall in.

By far the coolest new thing was TV. When the lady turned it on, I remember standing there with my mouth open, thinking "How did they get people in that box?" I was so amazed that I just had to put my face on the TV screen to take it all in. Of course, everyone laughed at me. I remember sitting on the couch with my mouth open and eyes glued to it, thinking to myself, "What is this?" I couldn't understand what the people were saying or what was going on. I just remember being amazed, sitting there watching it.

After my host was finished showing me around, she left to go into the kitchen and cook. I remember sitting in the family room watching as she prepared all kinds of African foods. I had never seen so many varieties of African food all at once before. While she was cooking, her granddaughter and I watched the magical box with people inside.

Soon more people came and brought clothes for me to put on. I changed out of my African clothes and put on what was going to be my new wardrobe. When I had changed, we left the building. We took with us all the food she had cooked. I don't remember where we went, I just remember eating until my heart was content. There were a lot of people and most of them tried to talk to me but I couldn't really talk to them, since I wasn't able to understand what they were saying.

While I was living with them, we had African foods and American foods. I discovered French fries and chicken nuggets. They quickly became my favorite American foods. In order to get American food the host's granddaughter and I would walk to another building, a McDonald's. Every time we got there, the granddaughter would say something and before long the people would just give us food and we would bring it home and eat it. Just like that, or so I thought.

As much as I enjoyed eating chicken nuggets and French fries, I did not like walking to McDonald's because it was cold. I believe when we came it was the season I now know as fall. I remember everywhere we went, there were piles of leaves and I was cold all the time, even when I was in the house. After a couple of days, my host mom and I went and visited one of the girls that lived close by so she and I could play. When we got there, she met someone that she knew and they started talking. We stood outside in the cold for a long time while they talked. Soon, I had to pee. I started doing my pee dance and pulling at her sleeve. But she paid no attention to me. In the village, I was taught to find a tree when I needed to go. So when she didn't acknowledge me, I looked around, saw a tree, and ran to it.

She must have noticed I was gone, because as soon as I started peeing she yanked me up. She started saying something while pointing at the tree and shaking her head. I couldn't understand why she was angry or what she was saying. It was probably something like "WE DO NOT PEE ON TREES HERE!" She literally scared the pee out of me because once we got in the house I had to borrow some pants!

While I was staying with her, she took me to a building called a church. I couldn't understand what was going on, what was being said, or the songs that were being sung. I just remember that everyone was happy in that building and there was food right after.

After a week of living with her and her family, we were taken to Staten Island, in New York City. All of us were moved into the Staten Island Hotel. While we were living there, we met other people who became a big part of our lives. Some are still part of our lives even today. Two of the people we met have since passed away, Uncle Joe and Uncle Carmine.

I remember the first time I met Uncle Joe. The other kids and I were all sitting in bed watching the magical box when he walked in. He was so tall and with his white hair he reminded me of the doctor at the Doctors Without Borders clinic, so for a while I was afraid of him. We started seeing Uncle Joe every day. He took us places where we met more and more people. Everywhere we went I was amazed by everything that was going on around me. Everyone we met was nice to us.

After a while, I got used to being around people with a skin color that was different from mine. When we landed in America, one of the things that fascinated me was all the different skin colors. I was amazed every time I walked the streets of New York.

The first time we met Uncle Carmine, we had to walk to his office. Uncle Joe had us all hold each other's hands while we walked there. Uncle Carmine was very friendly and hugged each of us. Then we played with toys and ate food while Uncle Joe and Uncle Carmine talked about us. We didn't see Uncle Carmine all that much before he passed away. There was a lady from Sierra Leone called Auntie Etta who also helped us. She spoke Krio, so she was a big help.

While we were in New York, our stories became public. There were always people around us taking pictures of us and asking us questions that we couldn't understand. Uncle Joe and the English-speaking adults in our group did most of the talking.

HOOK

Not long after coming to Staten Island, we were fitted for our prostheses. That was the reason we were brought to the United States in the first place. My first prosthesis was a pair of metal hooks that could open and close. It was hard getting used to it, and at first it was a little painful to wear. To put it on I had to put my stump in the prosthesis socket, run straps behind my shoulders, and put my left hand through another strap. The straps on the shoulders made the hooks open and close. I could open or close them by pulling my shoulders forward or backward.

I once made the mistake of wearing it on my bare skin. Throughout the day I was in so much pain because the straps pinched my skin every time I opened and closed the hooks. I learned to always wear a T-shirt underneath it then another one on top to hide the straps. Every time I put it on, I also had to wear a sock on my stump and sometimes it got really hot, especially in the summertime. At first, it felt really heavy. It took a lot of upper arm strength to open it. But once I got used to wearing it, I wore it every day.

Once we got our prostheses, our story became more widely known. We were in magazines and on TV. Our stories about the war in Sierra Leone and the effect it had on people became known nationwide. We even testified at the United Nations. Sometime after our testimony, the war ended in my country. We were only supposed to be in the U.S. for three months, enough time for each of us to get a prosthesis and other medical treatment, then go back. But our pictures and testimony at the U.N. became well known in Sierra Leone and not everyone there was pleased. In fact, some people threatened to kill us if we came back home. Because of that, the Staten Island Rotary Club, the group that brought us over, was afraid to send us back. After a while, they decided to help us apply for political asylum so we wouldn't have to go back as originally planned.

Life continued for us. We were meeting people and going places every day. Soon we met Auntie Nancy, a lady who played a big part in our lives. She became one of the people who volunteered to take us places. I remember when she introduced us to Halloween. She came by the hotel one day and showed us a catalog of costumes. Most of us couldn't understand what she was trying to tell us, but the adults in our group who spoke English told us she wanted us each to pick an outfit. I decided to dress as a doctor. I was so excited when we went shopping and I saw the doctor outfit. We were all invited to a Halloween costume party with other young kids, and at first everything was fine. I was proud of my costume and excited about the party until I saw all the scary things around me. The American kids were wearing costumes with fake blood dripping down from their faces and all over their clothes, but I didn't know the blood was fake. There were scary noises all over the house and people would jump out of nowhere to scare us. Everyone was having the time of their lives except for me. I didn't understand the fun in scaring people and playing with blood. That was the day I decided that Halloween was not for me.

After a couple of months, we started getting help with our English. Someone would come to the hotel and spend the day teaching us how to introduce ourselves, how to ask things like "Where is the bathroom?" and parts of the American culture like looking people in the eye when they were talking to us. In my village it was rude to look at adults directly in the eyes. I learned at an early age not to ever look at my grandmother in the eye when she was talking to me. She loved me, but she would not hesitate to knock the daylights out of me if I was ever eye to eye with her. It took a while to get used to looking at American adults in the eyes when they were talking to me.

We also worked on our handwriting by tracing letters and numbers. It was hard for me to form the letters with my left hand. Writing came easy to the other kids but I had to work extra hard on it. Part of my problem was that my brain thought I was still right-handed, but I didn't have a right hand! That made everything even harder.

We also started going to a college to work with college students. They mainly played with us so we could practice saying things in English and asking questions in English. My favorite part was getting to swim with them when we were done with lessons. It was a heated indoor pool and I liked it. The nice warm water felt good because I was always cold in New York. I could never put on enough clothes to keep myself warm. While learning how to swim, I realized quickly that I was not a floater but a sinker. The rest of the kids were able to learn to float, but not me. I sunk every time I tried. I made sure to stay far, far away from the deep end.

My first experience with snow was horrifying. We were going on one of our many outings. I was all bundled up with as much clothing as I was able to put on. Uncle Joe came to pick us up. By this time, we were able to say things like "Hi, Uncle Joe. How are you Uncle Joe?" And "I am fine." We put on our shoes, coats, and hats and out we went.

We stopped for a while to take in what was happening around us. We had never seen anything like snow before. Everything was white and there were more white flakes coming down from the sky. I remember standing out there looking up in the sky while Uncle Joe pointed and repeated the word "snow" over and over again. It was amazing to see but also very cold. We started walking to Uncle Joe's car, but before we got there I stepped into a deep pile of snow. When I lifted my foot, my shoe did not come with it. I was shocked when I felt the cold going up my leg. The whole thing came as such a surprise to me, that for a while I couldn't do anything but stand there with tears coming down my face. The rest of the gang realized that I wasn't with them, so they started calling for me, "Come on Fatu. Let's go!" I tried to move but I wasn't able. It felt like I was glued to the ground. Uncle Joe had to come pick me up and carry me back to the house to change my socks. This time I made sure my shoes were good and tight. After that, snow did not excite me anymore. It still doesn't even to this day.

Our first Christmas was eye-opening. There was much going on everywhere we went. I remember being amazed looking at the Christmas trees, the decorations, and the different-colored lights. We especially liked to see the decorations at night. Everything seemed magical to us. There was music in every store. And the gifts! None of us had ever received so many gifts. We went to many people's houses and each time there were presents for us and a lot of food. I didn't really get the whole concept of Christmas, but getting gifts and eating all that food made it my favorite holiday. For a while, I used to think the only things American people did were eat, have fun, and be nice to everyone.

In Staten Island, life was easy. There was enough to eat every day. People were taking care of us and taking us places. At night I was able to sleep with both my eyes closed. I wasn't worried about rebels coming after me. During the war, going to sleep was hard for me. I was always on edge, afraid that something bad was going to happen. I got used to sleeping with my ears alert, ready to run if I heard loud noises or screaming. Even though things weren't as bad in Freetown, there were still bad people roaming around the camp that could hurt us. My favorite times in the camp were when it rained during the night. I used to think no one would get out in the rain to hurt me. So every time it rained I could sleep more easily.

Even though I wasn't afraid of the rebel soldiers in Staten Island, it still took me a while to fall asleep peacefully at night sometimes. The unfamiliar noises bothered me. As good as life was, I still had trouble with anxiety. Since I couldn't understand what people were saying or what was going on around me, I was always jumpy if I heard loud voices. Even though I didn't think anyone was going to hurt me, I was uncomfortable being in new places or meeting new people. This was a problem because during our time in Staten Island we went to many new places and met many new people.

For example, we had the chance to meet President Clinton and his wife Hillary. I remember they came and shook each kid's hand. There were many other people with us that day. I couldn't understand why everyone was so excited to see them, or why everyone wanted to shake their hands. I was happy that they held my hand even though it was dirty and rough.

The next year we were placed in school. Our first school was a Catholic school. Auntie Nancy and the two ladies in our group took us shopping for school supplies and uniforms. That was a happy day for all of us kids. We were excited to get all those new things. I was 10 years old but was placed in second grade because I couldn't speak English and had never really had any education. It was hard sitting in class listening to directions that I couldn't understand. It took me a while to get comfortable being there. Since there wasn't anything for me to do, I spent most of my time just watching the other kids. They seemed happy all the time and even though we were wearing the same outfits, theirs always looked nicer on them. The girls' hair was always fixed so perfectly, their hands were always so clean, and their socks and shoes were always so neat and tidy. I felt out of place sitting in that classroom every day with my head down watching everybody else.

Just when I was beginning to believe New York was safe, 9/11 happened. We were in our classroom when the buildings were hit in Manhattan. While our teacher was talking to us, even though I couldn't understand everything she was saying, I could sense that something was badly wrong. I could see the fear in the other kids' eyes. Not long after, parents were coming to get their kids. I just sat there with no clue what was going on. All the kids in our group were asked to wait outside for our driver.

On the way home the streets were packed with cars. People were honking and yelling at each other. Some were running down the street trying to get home. By the time we made it home, I was on edge with fear. I didn't know what was happening around me. When we saw the news on TV, my fear increased even more. My first instinct was to run and hide. But where? Ever since we had come to the States, not once had I seen any forest. So for a couple of hours, I hid underneath the bed. I thought this might be the beginning of another bad experience, but thankfully we went back to school after a couple of days.

Close to the end of the school year things got a little bit better. The other kids started talking to me and including me. Some of them were very interested in my hook. They would come to me and ask me to open and close it. They thought it was cool that I could pick things up with it. I had learned to do a lot of things with my hook. I was able to tie my shoelaces or hold a pen or pencil or anything else that was small. At the end of the school year, we moved into a duplex. The three older guys had one side and the rest of us were in the other. I have some nice memories from that place.

I had my first experience riding a bike there. A couple who came to see us a lot brought a bike one day and started teaching us to ride. They made the whole thing look so easy that I was beyond excited to try it. I had never seen or played with anything like this in the village. Our fun there was climbing trees, kicking mangoes like soccer balls, fishing with the adults, chasing chickens, or running races to see who was fastest. We never had things like bikes, dolls, or anything fancy, so I was very excited to learn how to ride. At first, I had trouble moving my legs correctly, but I was determined to ride and after a couple falls and some bruises I thought I had learned enough to try it all by myself.

With my broken English, I told the man who was helping me to let go. At first I was unsteady, but I was riding! I was moving my feet as fast as I could and I liked the way it felt. I decided to go farther down the street. I didn't realize there was a slope. As I started going down I could hear everyone yelling "Stop, Fatu!" I tried to jump off the bike but my hook wouldn't open. I did everything I could to unhook myself. I even tried yelling at the hook but nothing happened. The bike and I just kept on going down and down. There is a reason my prosthesis was called a hook. It hooked onto that bike and it would not let go for anything! That was a ride I do not ever want to repeat. I don't think my head could take another hit like that. A couple of days later, the same couple brought us roller blades. Again I was excited to ride them, but it didn't take long before my excitement turned to "I hate these things!"

My favorite memory of that place, was going to the Staten Island Hospital to eat. That's where we were introduced to Uncle Andy. He was the chief of the hospital. Once in a while, we would go there to eat and we were allowed to eat whatever we wanted. I would eat and eat until my stomach hurt. When we first came to the United States, I would always eat everything that was put in front of me. I couldn't say no to food because I remembered being hungry during the war. I would always eat like it might be my last meal for a long time. I couldn't throw any food away. Everything went in my mouth.

The summer ended, and we went back to school. This time I had some help in the classroom. Someone sat with me and explained the instructions in a way I could understand. Once in a while someone else would take me out of the classroom to talk about how things were going, how I felt, and how I liked school. I used to hate having to sit down and talk with that lady. With my limited English, I couldn't explain to her how I really felt. I couldn't explain to her that I felt lost and alone, that I felt like I was in the wrong place or that I was still afraid that something bad would happen to me again, so most of the time I didn't say anything. I just sat there and played with the toys she brought with her and she did all the talking.

Some of the kids at school made things easier for us. They would play with us, sit with us in the lunchroom, and talk with us the way they would talk to their regular friends even though most of the time we couldn't really understand what they were saying. We were invited to birthday parties and other gatherings, so things were going okay in school. But we had other problems.

The two ladies that came with us told us there was a chance we might have to go back to Sierra Leone. This put fear in us because none of us wanted to go back, especially since we had been threatened with death if we returned. There were other questions, too. If we went back, how were we going to get our prostheses fixed if they broke? Who was going to replace them with larger ones when we outgrew them? There was a lot of debate about what to do with us, since our time of staying in the U.S. was almost up. Uncle Joe and other members of the Rotary Club fought hard for us to stay.

After a while, our request for political asylum was approved. That meant we could stay in the U.S. I remember that day talking to my grandmother on the phone telling her that I wasn't going back. I could tell in her voice that she was sad as she kept on repeating "Be good, Fatu. Be good."

After we got political asylum, stories and pictures made it into magazines and newspapers about us amputee kids from West Africa. The articles said that we needed to be adopted. One newspaper in Kentucky printed our story. A family named Litsey saw that article and came to visit us in New York. All seven of them came to our apartment. We were all introduced to each other, then Uncle Joe explained to them about our situation. I couldn't really understand everything he was saying, but he kept on repeating over and over the word adoption.

When I first met the Litseys, I thought they were just another family who would visit and never come back again. I was shy around them and didn't say much. A couple of weeks later I was told that I was going to visit them in Kentucky. During my Christmas break, I went for a one-week visit.

I remember being very scared of going. I had gotten used to being in the same room with white people, but I had never spent the night with them. I was scared, not knowing what was going to happen to me. For the first days of the visit, I was very uncomfortable being around them and I was also very shy about my stump. One night Mom was trying to help me with a bath. She tried to help me get out of my clothes and I was very quick to say "No, no, no. I will do it." I wasn't going to take my hook off until she was out of the bathroom. I was very uncomfortable about having her see my stump. I had this crazy idea in my head that my stump was too ugly for anyone to see.

The Litseys had five children by birth and had also just adopted two other girls from Sierra Leone, Sinnah and Sento. They had only been in the states a couple weeks before I came to visit the Litseys. I tried to talk to them in Timni, but they were too shy to talk to me. After my one-week visit, I went back to Staten Island and did not think about the Litseys again.

Later that year, one of the ladies that came with us sat me down and told me that I was going to live with the family I had visited. While she was telling me this, I remember not having any emotions. I wasn't afraid or unhappy. It just felt like something else I had to go through. I really didn't have much time to think about whether I wanted to live with the Litseys or not, because time was running out. If I wasn't adopted quickly I'd be sent into foster care. Most of the other kids were already with families. It was just me and one other girl who were left. In the spring of 2003, my new sister Rachel and my new mom came back to New York to bring me home. After a day of sightseeing, we got on the plane and it was "Bye-Bye, New York" and "Hello, Kentucky!"

WHITESVILLE

Being around the Litseys the second time was less uncomfortable. I was still shy about my hand but it didn't take long before I was walking around the house without my hook. By the end of summer things felt natural. My two African sisters and I met a lot of people. We were welcomed by everyone we met and soon everyone knew who we were.

We lived in a little town called Whitesville, in western Kentucky. Whitesville was very different from New York City. It was a lot quieter! In New York City, everywhere we went there were unexpected loud sounds. The loud sounds made it hard for me to live there in peace. Whitesville was also a lot greener than New York City. There were farm fields all around. It reminded me of my village. In Mafunta, everything turned green in the rainy season and nearly everything died in the dry season. In Whitesville there wasn't a dry season, but things would "die" in the winter.

Seeing green fields in the summer made me feel right at home. Even though farming was very different in my village, it was still nice to see corn and soy beans growing. Just like in my village, everyone knew everyone. Especially since my dad was a doctor in Whitesville, a lot of people knew my family. While living there, my two African sisters and I were the only black people around, but that was never a problem for us. Everyone came to love us.

I used to enjoy our trips into nearby Owensboro twice a week. Sometimes Mom would take us to do grocery shopping there. We would get into our van with excitement, and Mom would buy a bunch of groceries to take back with us. We went to church in Owensboro too, every Sunday.

One hard thing about living out in the country is, there is no turning back if you forget something. Every time we would go somewhere, I always managed to forget to bring something. I would ask my parents to turn back to get it, but every time the answer was "No, Fatu." It made my Sundays less enjoyable. I used to be obsessed with looking good every time I went to church and if I didn't have my lip gloss or earrings, it felt like my Sunday was ruined. After a while, Mom and pretty much everyone else in the family started asking me before we left home every Sunday if I had remembered everything.

Our house in Whitesville was on a hill close to the road. Across from us were two houses and another house was beside us. The people next to us had a field, but the field wasn't used for growing crops. Instead, it was where they kept their donkeys. Those donkeys were really friendly. They would eat out of our hands. The donkey field was close by our house, so we could hear them every time they made their "Hee Haw" noises. It could be annoying, hearing them night and day, but the way they smelled was worse. And since we were living close by, there were flies too. It drove one of my African sisters crazy. She never did like those donkeys, and we could never get her to eat outside because of those flies. I didn't feel strongly either way about the donkeys, but their "Hee Haw" noises were always very funny to me.

Before he went to the Marines, my big brother built us a tree house. We had some good times playing in that tree house. I felt like I was climbing trees again, even though it wasn't the same. We also had our own garden. I remember all of us helping in the garden. We mainly had to pull weeds, and Dad took care of everything else. In our garden, we planted tomatoes, bell peppers, sunflowers, and okra. We grew more okra than anything else. My two sisters and I loved okra because we ate it in Africa. The rest of the family loved it too.

When school started, I attended Whitesville Elementary School as a fourth grader. Being in fourth grade wasn't easy. Even though I was able to understand a little of what the teacher was saying, I still had trouble keeping up in class because I didn't have a good foundation in the subjects. I pretty much had to start from the basics.

I had an ESL (English as a Second Language) teacher who helped me in and out of the classroom. Sometimes I would skip recess to ask my teachers for help and as the year went by, some of the subjects started getting easier. With the help I was getting from my ESL teacher, I began to enjoy going to school. I was always eager to learn new things even though it was hard. I became friends with everyone in my classroom. All the students and all the teachers knew me. I was happy because I could finally say that I belonged.

But even though I felt accepted, I was still shy about letting my friends or anyone else in the school know that I only had one hand and wore a hook. I was so ashamed of my hook that I would wear long sleeve shirts to cover it. If the shirt sleeve wasn't long enough, I would stretch it until it was. It looked weird, having one stretched-out sleeve, but that did not bother me as much as having my friends see my hook. I would wear long sleeve shirts throughout the year. In the summertime it drove me crazy wearing a long sleeve shirt in the heat, but still I did it.

Being shy about my hand kept me from enjoying a lot of things. My friends sometimes would invite me to sleepovers and pool parties but I would always say no. The idea of showing them that I only had one hand was beyond embarrassing.

I almost let the fact that I only had one hand stop me from playing sports. I remember one time telling my parents that I wanted to play soccer. I had always enjoyed running and kicking things. When I asked them, they signed me up. I was very excited until they told me I couldn't play with my hook on. Well, there was no way I was going to go out there running around with my stump showing. The excitement of playing soccer was gone after that and I told them I didn't want to play after all. But that night, they sat me down and told me that I couldn't go on being shy about my amputation. I knew what they were saying was right, but the idea of going out there with my stump and having people look at me made me feel very uncomfortable.

After the talk I decided to give it a try, but I was still wearing long sleeve shirts out on the field to cover my stump. I enjoyed playing, just like I thought I would. While I was out there playing, I really didn't pay too much attention to my hand. Yes, people were looking at me, but I was having too much fun to really care. Before long, I became known as the fastest player on the team. Parents enjoyed watching me play and I got along pretty well with my teammates.

During my fifth grade year, my parents talked with me about getting another prosthesis. It was going to be nicer-looking than my hook. It would look more like a hand and be battery operated, with fingers that would open and close almost like a real hand. That was the best news I'd had since coming to live with them! I was beyond excited.

Not too long after, they took me to a prosthesis office to be measured and to choose a skin tone for my new hand. They called some weeks later; my hand was ready! I was very excited as I walked into the office and literally jumped out of my chair when the man showed it to me. It was a perfect fit and the skin tone was similar to mine! He showed me how to move my stump to open and close the fingers. It wasn't hard to learn. To open the fingers, I would pretend I was bending my wrist up. To close the fingers, I would pretend I was bending my wrist down. On the day I got it, I was so excited that the whole ride home the only thing I could talk about was how I was going to paint my fingernails, hold a fork and a pencil, and stop wearing long-sleeved shirts. The list went on and on.

On the same day I got my hand I had a soccer game, and was excited to wear my new hand out on the field. We were about to leave the house when Mom told me that I couldn't take my hand. I was so sad, I cried hard as we sat in my room while she listed all the reasons why I couldn't wear it while playing. She said that even though it looked like a hand, it was heavy and hard and if I wore it out there I could hurt somebody. Also, it was very expensive and might get broken during the game. I was very sad that I had to leave it at home, but I could see that Mom was right. The way I used to play, my team and the other team could all have ended up at the hospital. I was fearless going after the soccer ball. So once again, I had to go out on the field five fingers short.

I liked my new prosthesis much better than my old one. It was less painful to wear and easier to use. I wore it through my fifth, sixth, and seventh grade years.

I skipped eighth grade because I was two grades behind and didn't like being the oldest kid in all of my classes. I got along well with my classmates, but felt out of place because of my age. My parents and my teachers decided it would be better for me to be with kids closer to my age. So when the eighth-graders went to visit Daviess County High School, I went with them. I remember sitting on the bus. All of the eighth graders were looking at me funny because they knew I was only a seventh grader. One girl asked me why I was on the bus. I told her I was skipping eighth grade, and her next question was "How smart *are* you?" I didn't answer. I was happy to start high school. I knew I would need to study extra hard, but I was more than willing.

Being adopted by the Litseys greatly changed my life, but it changed their lives too. I don't really remember the whole adoption process because I was young and didn't know what was happening, but a couple of years after they adopted my two sisters and me, my parents decided that God was calling them into missions. My dad told me once that adopting us was the beginning of God calling them to be missionaries. Our stories and our lives opened their eyes to the healing Jesus Christ can bring to a person's life. My two sisters and I were very broken kids. Sinnah and Sento had trouble trusting people and allowing people to love them. I also still had some fears that I was keeping to myself.

My dad decided to sell his medical practice and become a missionary. We all had good memories of living in Whitesville, and we were all sad to say goodbye, but we sold our house at the end of my seventh grade year, and our next adventure began.

BACK TO AFRICA

We moved to Tennessee so Dad could go to Johnson Bible College (now it is known as Johnson University). I started ninth grade in Knoxville. When we moved, my oldest brother Matthew was in the Marines and my sister Rachel was a student at Johnson, living in a dorm there. That left only six of us kids still living together in our new house.

I don't really know what happened inside me, but when we moved to Tennessee, wearing my prosthesis out in public didn't seem so important. I started going out without even thinking about it. I went through the entire summer without wearing it. School started and I went the first day without it, then the next day, and before I knew it I was going to school every day without it.

Ninth grade was tough, but I was able to join

some school activities. I joined the soccer team and the track team and I was also in ROTC. It didn't really bother me when people stared at me, or that once in a while somebody would ask how I lost my hand. I was proud to wear my soccer and track uniforms without long sleeves.

I really enjoyed my freshman year. I had fun because I stopped worrying about my hand. Trying to keep up with everything in my classes was hard, but accepting who I was made everything OK. It made me happy. Very happy. As the year went by, I became known to my friends and teammates as the one-handed girl, and I was cool with that!

My sophomore year, we moved to Dallas so my parents could get more missionary training. While we were there, Dad homeschooled all six of us. We studied on our own but he was there to help us if we needed it. I enjoyed living in Dallas, especially the weather.

I became friends with all the young people at our church. By that time, I couldn't have told you where my prosthesis was if you asked me. Between the moves, I somehow lost the charger that went with it, so the hand was dead. And since I wasn't wearing it anyway, I didn't see the point of getting another charger for it. I had learned to do so many things with just my stump. I could cut and paint my nails, tie my shoes, do dishes, and cut food. Having a prosthesis had been great at first, but now I was able to do more without it!

The next year we moved to Quebec, Canada, because my parents needed to learn French before going to Africa. While we were there, the rest of the kids went to public schools but I attended language school with my parents. Living in Quebec was nice in the summertime. We did a lot of sightseeing and ate a lot of baguettes, but one of my favorite things to eat there was liver pâté on crackers. We often played soccer with the other kids whose parents were in the same language school.

It was nice until winter came and then I was ready to get out of that country. The snow came down nonstop every single day. I became so tired of snow that even the idea of getting up in the morning made me sick. Even with all that snow the local people were still out and about, but it was hard for us. My brothers and sisters would walk through high snow to get to school and my parents and I would drive on ice or snow or slush every day. We had snow throughout winter and that to me was not cool!

In 2009, the eight of us moved to Guinea, West Africa. At first, all three of us African girls were nervous about going back because we had bad memories of the war. I wasn't sure how the whole thing was going to play out. Was I going to be treated differently due to the fact that I only had one hand? Would people think that my situation was a punishment from God? But when we got there, my whole family and I were accepted by the people. I found out living in Africa this second time gave me a lot of peace.

We became good friends with the other missionaries that were already there and we also became good friends with a lot of the local people. At first, some of the local kids were afraid of my hand. Every time they came over and saw my stump they would run home crying. I couldn't really understand why they were so scared, but after a while they got used to me. In fact, eventually they started touching and even squeezing my stump when they came.

We had a good time while living in Guinea. Every other day all the missionary kids would get together to play games and once a week the local kids would come over to our house and play soccer. We tried to introduce them to new games, but soccer was always their number one choice. It didn't take long before everybody knew about my two sisters and me and why we were living with white people.

Although Guinea and Sierra Leone are neighboring countries, Guinea was different from Sierra Leone. The dishes people ate were different and the way people dressed was also different. Everybody there knew about the war in Sierra Leone. In fact while we were there, I learned that a lot of people from Sierra Leone fled to Guinea during the war.

My family and I lived in a small town, but not as small as Mafunta. There were some modern things like cars, trucks, battery-operated radios, and other things that Mafunta didn't have. But many things were similar. There were mango trees, our neighbor had a papaya tree, and we ate a lot of avocados and bananas. The weather was the same too, hot and dry in the dry season and hot and wet in the rainy season. My family and I ate things that were familiar to me, like fried termites. We also cooked mangoes, a simple and filling meal we ate quite often while I was a little kid. It was nice being back in Africa after all those years.

In Guinea we didn't need to trap animals for meat. On market days the town butcher would kill a cow and Mom would buy beef from him. It was very tough, so we would grind it before we cooked it. That was a lot of fun, the whole family working together and joking around as we prepared our meat. We also bought live chickens to kill and eat. We could even buy frozen chickens in the capital a few times a year. We would can them in jars and eat them later.

While we were there, all six of us were home-schooled again. Before we left the states, my parents bought GED materials for me to study while I was there. At first Mom and Dad taught my brothers and sisters, but later we had a teacher come to help. I studied on my own and only asked for help from my parents when I needed it.

While we were living in Guinea, Mom and all of us girls dressed like the other local women and girls. In the Muslim culture it is considered inappropriate for a female to show legs and uncovered head, so we wore head coverings and long skirts or dresses whenever we left the house.

I am glad that I went to Guinea with my family, because for a while I was getting too comfortable living the American life. I was starting to forget the African way of living: the hot sun, working all day, and walking miles and miles to get places. No, we didn't have to work all day in the hot sun or walk miles and miles in Guinea, but seeing village kids younger than me doing it made me think back to when I did.

Going back and seeing the way people lived also made me realize how much my life had changed. I didn't have to worry about where I was going to get food any more, in fact I had forgotten what it was like to go hungry. I didn't have to worry about my safety because I knew as long as I was with my parents I would be safe. I really didn't have to worry at all. The only thing I had to do was get up every morning to study for my GED, so I could finish high school and start planning for my future. How crazy is that? My life had completely changed from almost dying under that tree as a hopeless little kid, to asking myself what

I wanted to do with the rest of my life! I became friends with a lot of village girls younger than me, who were already married. They had no education and no choice other than to work their fields and care for their children.

Living in Guinea was a life-changing experience for all of us. My non-African family also learned a lot. We learned how to get things done using what we had. For example, killing snakes with rocks and sticks was something we did a lot in Mafunta. In Guinea, my whole family learned how to kill snakes with rocks. It wasn't easy but together we got the job done. In Mafunta, we did our laundry by beating our wet clothing on big rocks, using our hands to squeeze out the water, then spreading it out on the grass to dry. In Guinea we also did our laundry by hand using a tub, washboard, and wringer. There was some complaining, but we worked together and our clothes were clean!

We learned a little bit of the local language to get by. My parents learned more of the language than we kids did, because their main focus was to talk to people about Jesus.

HOME

After two years in Guinea, my sister Laura and I came back to the states while the rest of the family stayed in Africa for one more year. I lived with some friends of my parents. While living with them, I took some more classes to prepare for my GED exam. It wasn't easy, but I really wanted my GED and I studied night and day to get ready for it. In the spring of 2011, I took the exam and passed it! That summer I started taking classes to get my license as a Certified Nursing Assistant.

Soon I was working as a CNA and also taking classes at our community college. It was difficult taking those college courses and working, but I worked hard and studied hard. At that point I was only taking the basic classes. I still wasn't sure what I wanted to study, but I could tell being a CNA would be difficult to do with only one hand for the rest of my life.

In May 2012, the rest of the family came back home to Kentucky. Dad and I started talking about what I wanted to do next. At first I liked the idea of becoming a social worker, because I enjoy working with people but my Dad thought that I might not like it as much. A week later he came to me again with the idea of becoming an occupational therapy assistant.

At first I had no idea what an occupational therapy assistant was, but he gave me a brief description of it and I really liked the idea. I started looking into it and that summer I went to observe an occupational therapist. After talking to her and seeing what she did, I decided that occupational therapy assistant might be a good fit for me. I liked the idea of teaching a person how to do things after being disabled after a stroke or an accident. By the end of the summer we had gotten a clear picture of what college courses I needed to take and what college to attend.

In the fall of that year, I started taking more science classes. They were the hardest classes I had ever taken, but I was able to get through them with help from my family, especially my dad. By the end of 2013, I had taken all the classes I needed to apply to a college with an OTA program. I was accepted into the program at the University of Southern Indiana.

In July of 2014, I moved to Evansville, Indiana and started class. The program was only a year and a half, so it was intense, a lot of classes in a short time.

The first semester was difficult but after that things got easier. In December 2015, I graduated with an associate's degree as an occupational therapy assistant.

LOOKING BACK

Now let me go back and explain how the war started. In the 1990s the government in Sierra Leone wanted to collect taxes on diamonds that were mined there, but some powerful people did not want to pay the diamond taxes. At that time unregistered, untaxed diamonds could be sold to the major European diamond merchants with no questions asked about where the diamonds originated. Since Sierra Leone's army was not strong, a group of greedy evil men created a rebel army of their own to take control of the mines in my country. The point of the war was money.

Their army was brutal. It terrorized the people of my country, even in villages like Mafunta where there weren't any diamonds. The rebels did unimaginable things to people. They would enter a town and do whatever they wanted. They would give a young boy a gun and tell him to shoot his family members, then take the boy and force him to become a rebel soldier too. In fact, I remember the guy who cut my hand was just a boy, maybe in his early teens. They would give these boys drugs so they would fight fearlessly. They would also capture village girls for their pleasure. Nobody was able to stand up to them and fight because everybody was fearful of them.

The night they entered my village was the beginning of us running away from them. It was hard moving from one place to another just to stay alive, not knowing when the rebels would discover us. And it was hard not knowing where to run when the rebels came. I remember the times they discovered us, everyone always would go crazy trying to run away and sometimes most of us were lucky to get away.

As a child, I didn't know what war was, what diamonds were, what a plane was, or even what a gun was. I never really did understand any of that. But the war I didn't understand changed everything for me, especially the day that machete hit my hand.

Having only one hand is not easy. I go through challenges daily. But over the years, I have learned that being patient, being strong, and having a good attitude in whatever situation I am in has helped me accomplish many things. I don't let having one hand stop me from doing the things I want to do.

I am learning every day how to do things with one hand. Sometimes it's easy and other times it takes time and patience to master a task. Every day I was in the OTA program, I had to develop new strategies to do things. We did a lot of splinting, which involved cutting material with scissors. I learned to hold the paper between my stump and my knee to cut out the pattern. I was very slow but I got the job done. When I needed to learn how to give CPR, I found a way that worked for me. Once again I was slow, but I got my CPR certification just like everybody else. When I needed to learn the proper way to transfer patients, I mastered that skill too. It wasn't easy trying to lift someone using only one hand, but I learned.

Over the years I have accepted that there is nothing I can do about having one hand, but there are days when I still feel embarrassed, especially when I am around new people. One day in OTA school we had a simulation class where all the health care students came together to practice on mannequins to get us ready for medical emergencies. My job as an OTA was to do CPR while everybody else did the other medical procedures before the mannequin "died." When we got there and we started working, all the other students were moving so fast and doing everything so quickly that I got scared. I was embarrassed to be struggling to do CPR and slowing everyone down, so I moved out of the way and watched while everybody else worked. It was humiliating standing there watching. There are still times like that, but not as many.

There are also times when I feel out of place, confused, and lost in ways that don't relate to my hand. I want to make sense of everything that happened to me as a child, but that will never happen in this life. For example, I don't know my birth family's health history. My answer will always have to be "I don't know" whenever I'm asked about it. I don't even know the names of my birth parents or any of my blood siblings. I will never truly know how old I am, because there is no record of my birth. When I came to the U.S., I was simply assigned a birthday. I will never be able to explain these parts of my story to my kids. But thanks to God my kids are someday going to hear about my new family history.

Being adopted can make you feel out of place. You come into a new family and you don't know if you will fit in with them. For a while I felt out of place when I was with my grandparents, aunts and uncles, and cousins. I didn't know how to behave around them, but it didn't take long before I felt accepted. The love and care they gave me made being in my family a good thing. It was all because God was watching out for my African sisters and me. I thank God for the family he carefully picked out for us.

But being adopted into a white family can produce some awkward moments. There have been times when my white brothers and sisters introduced Sinnah, Sento, and me as their sisters and got confused looks in return. They have to tell people their African sisters were adopted. Just as a joke, I have sometimes told people that my white brothers and sisters were adopted into my family. No one gets the joke until they meet our parents.

I turned 16 in Texas and I wanted to learn to drive. I went to apply for a learner's permit but the lady at the office wouldn't let Dad sign for me without proving he was my Dad. In Africa, the police would stop us when they saw Sinnah, Sento, and me in a car with our white family. Dad would have to show our papers and explain we were adopted.

Because we were adopted into a white family, my sisters and I know more about white American culture then we do about West African culture. If we had been adopted by a West African family, we might know more about our birth culture. But it didn't turn out that way. We are constantly surrounded by white people, so to us it just feels natural. All the places we have lived over the years, except for Guinea, have been white communities. The majority of my closest friends are white. There are times when I feel out of place being the only black girl in my group, but I have learned to quickly dismiss those feelings. This is the life God has given me. I am not ashamed of it and do not wish that things had turned out differently. I am exactly where God wants me to be. I am loved by my friends and my family.

There will always be questions I can't answer. For example, I was so sad when I didn't get on that truck with my uncle. But now I wonder what would have happened to me if I had climbed on. Would I even be alive today? What happened to all those people that went in the truck? Did they ever make it to Freetown or were they attacked on the road? If they were attacked, did any of them survive? All I know is I never saw any of them ever again. Not in the camp or anywhere. Did God save my life that day? I also sometimes wonder if I could have escaped the rebels that last time if I hadn't looked back and tripped. Maybe someday when I am united with my creator I will get my answers. But I already can see that he has turned something evil into something wonderful.

It is amazing how some of the things I was afraid of turned out to be blessings. The big white birds that I was afraid of for so long brought me to this country. The white people that I was afraid of are now my parents, family, and friends. I don't understand, but I can't complain. Since that awful day happened, I have faced one obstacle after another, but through them all I have gained so much.

Sometimes I still can't believe what God has done in my life. From so much evil has come so much good. Things were out of my control, but nothing was ever out of God's control. When I was on the brink of dying, I didn't ask him to save my life, but he did. He did it because I am his child and because he knew my future. I didn't ask for the life he has given me now, but he gave it.

The war took away my childhood and everything I knew. I don't know why I had to go through it. There have been days when I hated having to remember something that had happened to me. I wished that I could forget it all and never have to think about somebody cutting me and leaving me to die, never have to think about me walking day after day looking for help, never have to think about being left alone sitting under a tree night and day waiting to die.

But now, the little girl who almost died under that tree is full of life. The little girl who had to beg all day for food now has plenty to eat every day. The little girl who couldn't even spell her own name at the age of 10 has now graduated from college. The little girl who didn't have a future now has so much to live for. The little girl who felt like she was all alone now realizes she was never alone.

It has been 20 years since I lost my hand, my home, and everything I knew. Every time I have trouble doing something because of having one hand, I remember the war. Every time I look at my stump I remember, and every time I see the scars on my body, I remember. I will always remember, but I like the person I have become, the funny, outgoing, hard-working, sarcastic (and of course good-looking) human being God created me to be.

But even to this day, I am emotionally and physically affected by the war. There are things that still put fear in me. Every time I hear loud plane noises my heart skips a beat. Every time I hear unexpected loud sounds I can't help but jump. On the 4th of July, even though I know what is going to happen and give myself a pep talk, whenever I hear the sound of fireworks, my palm sweats and my heart pounds out of my chest. These are fears that will probably stay with me the rest of my life, but I can't let these fears stop me from going out there and becoming the person that God created me to be. I can't hide myself from the world and live in fear.

What I went through could have destroyed me if I had let it. And for a little while I *was* letting it. When I used to be shy about having one hand, it took a lot of joy out of me. That made it hard to be around other people. I'm glad God didn't let me continue down that road.

MORE THAN A SURVIVOR

I have written about many changes in my life, but the most important by far was discovering Jesus Christ. For a long time, I was angry with God that he let me go through so much trouble. I was angry that as powerful as he is, he let bad people take so much from me. I was not on good terms with God. I would go to church because my parents went and I had to go too, but deep inside I was hurt and angry.

That all changed when I decided to give my pain to him and learned how to forgive. It started in the spring of 2014. God started talking to my heart about sharing my story with the world. For a long time I had tried to forget the evil that had come to me in Africa. I had pretended for years that what I went through as a child hadn't affected my life, that if I just

111

continued to smile and be happy my life would be okay. But as we all know, God can`t be fooled. He knew that my happiness wasn't real. He knew what I needed. Pretending was no longer an option. If I was going to truly become one of His followers, I had to let go of the wounded Fatu and make peace with my childhood experience. I had to face that awful experience once again for healing to happen.

That spring I started to write down everything I could remember, but it was so painful to recall all those memories that I really didn't write for long. I soon went back to pretending again. But as the year went on, my fears of loud noises and being in places where I couldn't easily escape started to get worse. It was the summer of 2015 when I reached a turning point. My family and I had gone to the riverfront downtown for an airshow. At first the loud airplane sounds made me a little bit nervous, but after a while I started to enjoy the show. I was cheering and clapping with everyone else. But when I got up to find the restroom, an airplane suddenly flew low over the crowd. When I heard its thundering sound and the crowd yelling, I froze with fear. My first thought was something bad was going to happen. I stood there for a while with my heart jumping out of my chest watching the rest of the crowd cheer. That was the day the memory of the first attack came to the surface of my mind. When we got home, I sat down to write about that terrible night and after that everything started to just come up from my memory. All my past was coming back and I could no longer keep it in.

As I continued to write about my old life, I came to realize that I had never really presented my anger and fears to God. I was keeping everything inside and had never once asked him for help. As the year went by, I started presenting my pain to him and asking him to help me deal with it. But his way of helping was not what I expected. He helped me remember things I thought I had forgotten. It was during this process of remembering that I slowly began to see how he had been with me through everything and had been moving my life forward the whole time. I realized how much he had already helped me and how much help I still needed from him. I began asking him not just to give me peace, but to bring good from all the bad.

He also helped me understand that I needed to forgive the people who took so much from me for healing to happen. But how could I do such a difficult thing? That's when I first started to see something in the life of Jesus that I had missed before. Jesus had also been mistreated, but he had forgiven the very ones who had mistreated him. He said that anyone who wanted to follow him would need to forgive that way too.

Forgiving is one of the hardest things to do, but it is also how we are set free. It wasn't easy for me to forgive the soldier who cut my hand. I didn't even know his name, but in order for me to move on with my life I had to let go of the pain I had been holding inside for so long and the only way to do that was to forgive him. As I did so, I came to realize that he also had lost a lot from that war. He himself was just a boy. He probably didn't feel like he had much control over his life either. He probably was taken away from his home and his family. Maybe he had been forced to take drugs and do horrible things. Who knows what they might have forced him to do before he cut my hand? Or after. In a way, the war took more from him than it took from me. He has to live with the memory of what he did. Sometimes I wonder if he is still alive. If he is, does he have peace now? Has he found the forgiveness of God? I wish I could tell him that I have forgiven him. I pray God will somehow let him know.

I realized I also had to forgive the people who started the war in the first place, but this was much harder. They had let themselves be controlled by the prince of evil so completely that they thought the money they would make from those diamonds was worth all the misery and suffering they caused so many people. I couldn't feel sorry for them like I did for the boy who cut me, but I forgave them too.

After that, their control over my life was over. I probably will never understand why anyone would do what they did. But today I find myself thanking God, not only for the new life he has given me, but also for the old one. I thank him for the peace and blessings he has given me, and also for the sadness and suffering. Without the bad, the good wouldn't have happened. Even more, now I can see that I can help people in ways I could never have if I hadn't been through all those bad things.

I hope my story has encouraged you to trust God's wisdom in your life too. I hope that through my story you are able to see that even though we don't have complete control of our lives, God has everything under control. He has your best interest in mind. When the time is right, he will give you the help you need to face your struggles. He was always providing everything I needed just at the right time. When I needed water to drink, the rain came even though it was dry season. When I was wandering in the forest and had lost so much blood, somehow I always managed to rest safely at night and get back up the next day. Even those maggots that disgusted me so much were helping me. They were cleaning my stump by eating my dead flesh. And when I needed surgery for my hand, God somehow got me to the Doctors Without Borders clinic in Freetown. God was helping me all along, but I didn't know it. Amazing. And his care didn't stop then. When I came to the states I didn't know anybody, but I was well taken care of. He put me into a family who would lead me to him. And when it was finally time for me to face my childhood experiences, he brought people into my life to help me.

I had learned about a Christian group called Young Life through some friends that volunteered there. They would post videos and pictures of them doing crazy fun things with high school kids in our town as they taught them about Jesus. It never crossed my mind to join. One day we had a big thunderstorm and I volunteered to go help some of these friends clear some fallen trees at the house of Chris and Ashley, the leaders of Young Life in our town. Ashley and I worked alongside each other that day, and she asked questions about my life. We talked and joked with each other. I started seeing them at our church and we became friends. After a while, Chris approached me about the possibility of joining the Young Life group. We talked for a while about what Young Life is all about and I became interested in it. By the end of summer 2016, I was a Young Life volunteer at a local high school. I started meeting with the other Young Life volunteers and we all became good friends. That happened just at the same time I was writing my story down. With their help and encouragement, I began to deal with my experience and see how God had been working in my life.

One of the teachers at the high school where I volunteer asked if I would be willing to come talk to his English class. They had just read a book called "A Long Way Gone" about a child soldier in the same war. The teacher wanted someone who had actually been in the war to talk to his students. I wasn't sure if I was ready to be in front of people talking about my story. After talking to my Young Life friends and praying about it, though, I decided to do it. I put together a PowerPoint and with their help, I presented my story for the first time to a group of high school students. I could tell my story helped the students understand that the war affected real people, not only characters in a book.

That is my journey so far. I lost much, but thanks to God I have gained even more. I have survived many things, but I am more than just a survivor. Jesus is teaching me not just how to survive the evil in this world, but how to overcome evil. And not just the evil that touches me, but the evil that touches other people's lives as well. I can see that He is using my suffering to bring His blessing to other people. That has been my ultimate healing. My plan is to follow Him forever. I hope you will too.

"I have told you these things, so that in me you may have peace. In this world you will have trouble. But take heart! I have overcome the world."

-Jesus in John 16:33 (NIV)

Made in the USA
San Bernardino, CA
24 August 2017